Penguin Books
CHARLES HARPUR: SELECTED POETRY AND PROSE

Michael Ackland is a lecturer in English at Monash University, and is also Director of the Centre for General and Comparative Literature there. He has published a number of articles on Charles Harpur, and his place in Australian literature.

CHARLES HARPUR:
SELECTED
POETRY AND PROSE

Edited by Michael Ackland

Penguin Books

Penguin Books Australia Ltd,
487 Maroondah Highway, PO Box 257
Ringwood, Victoria 3134, Australia
Penguin Books Ltd,
Harmondsworth, Middlesex, England
Penguin Books,
40 West 23rd Street, New York, NY 10010, USA
Penguin Books (Canada) Limited,
2801 John Street, Markham, Ontario, Canada L3R 1B4
Penguin Books (NZ) Ltd,
182-190 Wairau Road, Auckland 10, New Zealand

First published by Penguin Books Australia, 1986
Published with the assistance of the Monash University Publications Committee

Copyright © this collection and introduction, Michael Ackland 1986

All Rights Reserved. Without limiting the rights under copyright reserved above, no part of this publication may be reproduced, stored in or introduced into a retrieval system, or transmitted, in any form or by any means (electronic, mechanical, photocopying, recording or otherwise), without the prior written permission of both the copyright owner and the above publisher of this book.

Typeset in Goudy Old Style by Leader Composition Pty. Ltd.
Made and printed in Australia by
Dominion Press-Hedges & Bell

CIP

Harpur, Charles, 1813-1868.
Charles Harpur, Selected poetry and prose.

ISBN 0 14 007588 7.

I. Ackland, Michael, 1951– . II. Title.
A828.109

To the memory of my parents, Michele and Rayden

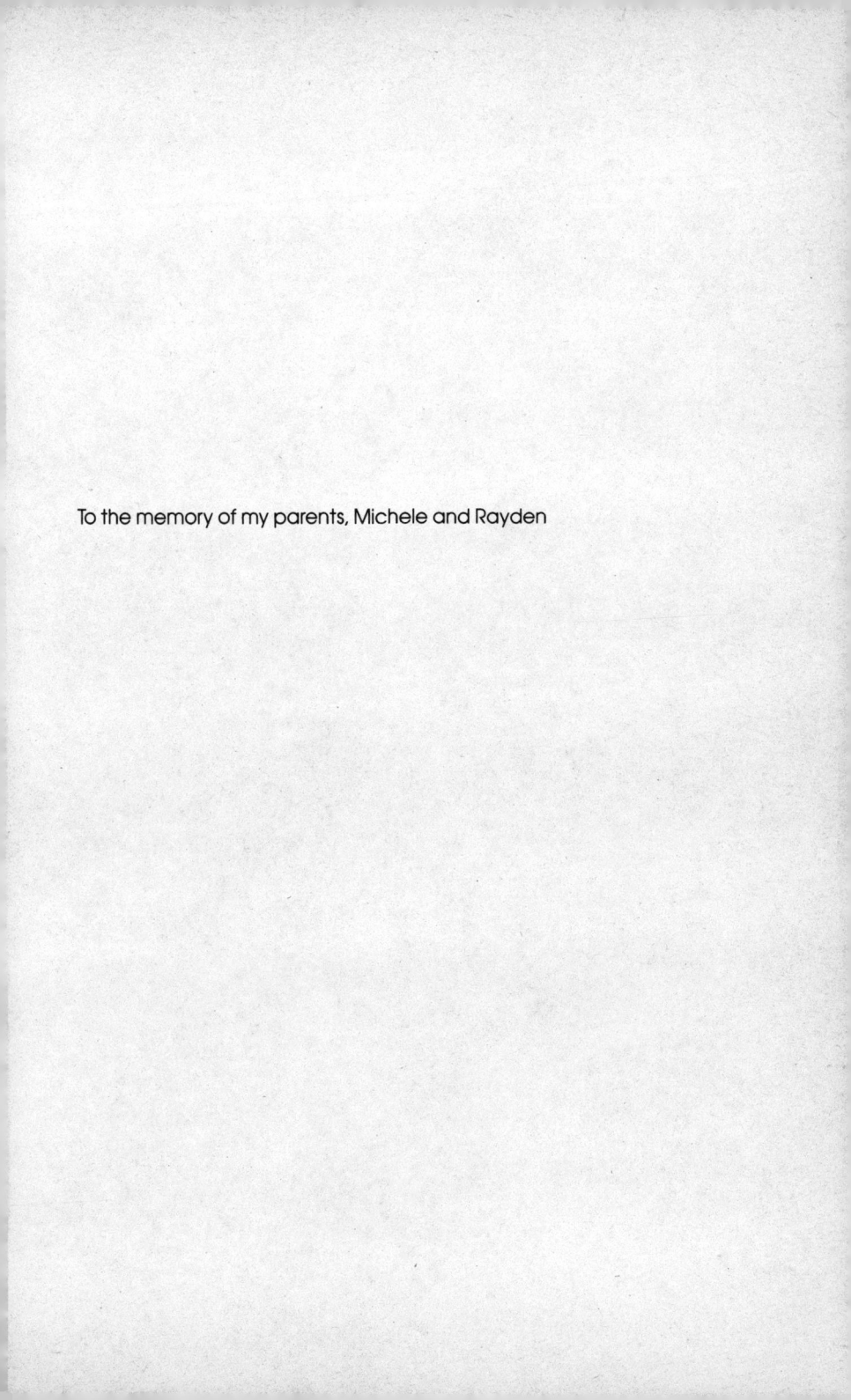

Contents

Introduction

• 1 • ON INDIVIDUAL AND NATIONAL DESTINY • 7

Charles Harpur – His Own Epitaph	9
The Dream by the Fountain	9
Final Note to the Miscellaneous Poems	12
from Rosa or Sonnets of Love	13
Note to The Lass of Eulengo	14
To the Sonnet on the Fate of Poetic Genius in a Sordid Community	16
To Myself, June 1855	17
Note to a Republican Lyric	18
This Southern Land of Ours	19
A Note on the Australian-born Whites from The Kangaroo Hunt	20
The Tree of Liberty	21
Finality	23
from The True Finality	25
Self-Liberty	28
Humanity	28

• 2 • ON POETS AND POETRY • 31

My Own Poetry	33
Australia's First Great Poet	34

from Harpur's Lecture on Poetry	34
Bible Poetry and Piety	39
Talent and Genius	41
Wordsworth's Poetry	42
Early and Late Art	42
Review of a Poem by Kendall	43
To Twank	43
Modern Poetry	44
from The Nevers of Poetry	44
from Finish of Style	44
The Perfect Poet	45
Andrew Marvell	45
To the Criticlings of Doggreldom	47
Poetical Egotism	47
from Harpur's Lecture on Poetry	49
The Tower of the Dream	50

• 3 • ON SOCIAL AND SPIRITUAL ISSUES •   67

Words *Are* Deeds	69
Asinine Loyalty and Abject Patriotism	69
True and False Glory	70
Wellington	71
Edmund Burke	71
On the Repeal Movement in Ireland	73
Whatever Is, Is Right	74
A Bit of Prose in the Vein and after the Manner of the Hon. Robert Boyle	75
Satire	75
Marvellous Martin	76
from The Temple of Infamy	79
A Roguish Epigram	80
from Sonnets Dedicated to Australian Senators	80
from Bits	81
The Big (Bygone) Claims of the Big Squatters	82
Bush Justice	84
A Splendid is Never a Happy Land	84
On the Proposed Recurrence to Transportation	85

Aboriginal Death Song	86
My Sable Fair	87
Charity	88
The Great Fish of the Sea (See)	90
Providential Design	91
Note to Have Faith	91
from The Witch of Hebron: A Rabbinical Legend	92
from Note to The Death of Shelley	99
Life and Death	101
Happiness and Faith	102
The World and the Soul	103
Note to the poem called Geologia	109
The Silence of Faith	110

• 4 • ON NATURE AND HUMAN RESPONSE •   111

Life Without and Within	113
A Similitude	113
A Flight of Wild Ducks	113
A Summer Night Scene	115
The Spouse of Infinitude	115
Note to the poem Early Summer	116
Early Summer	116
A Mid-Summer Noon in the Australian Forest	117
Dawn in the Australian Forest	119
Names of Colonial Birds	120
The Scenic Part of Poetry	121
A Coast View	122
The Bush Fire	125
Preface to The Kangaroo Hunt	131
A Storm in the Mountains	134
The Creek of the Four Graves	141
Poetic Descriptions of Violent Death	150
Eden Lost	151

• 5 • CORRESPONDENCE •   153

Charles Harpur to Henry Parkes, 21 March 1844	155
Charles Harpur to Nicol D. Stenhouse, 2 July 1859	157

Charles Harpur to Nicol D. Stenhouse, 12 November 1859	159
Henry Kendall to Charles Harpur, 25 September 1862	159
Charles Harpur to Henry Kendall, 9 November 1863	161
Henry Kendall to Charles Harpur, 29 April 1865	162
Charles Harpur to Henry Kendall, 10 June 1866	163
Charles Harpur to Henry Kendall, 7 July, 1866	164
Charles Harpur to Henry Kendall, 19 January 1867	165
Charles Harpur to Henry Kendall, 15 October 1867	166
Sources	168
Further Reading	169

INTRODUCTION

Charles Harpur is now acknowledged to be our most important colonial poet, but it was not always so. In his own lifetime, Harpur attracted both sincere praise and downright abuse. Among his friends he could number the future Colonial Secretary and Premier, Henry Parkes, the literary Maecenas of Sydney, Nicol Stenhouse, and the gifted native youth, Daniel Deniehy; all of whom hailed him as a writer of genius. Their encouragement, however, was more than counterbalanced by contemporary derision and incomprehension. The first survey of Australian writing, G. B. Barton's *Literature in New South Wales* (1866), stated flatly that 'the greater part of his compositions will never command much admiration'; and other writers have echoed Barton in finding Harpur's verse unmusical, his diction awkward, and the high opinion he held of his own productions to be absurd. The poet for his part responded bitterly to contemporary attacks, and repeatedly asserted both his mental superiority to and his moral alienation from his materially-obsessed fellows:

In short, my name and fame up to this moment, except as bye words in the mean mouths of such defamers and detractors, are utterly blanks in their day and generation; – and I conclude, therefore, that either I am unworthy of my country and countrymen, or my countrymen are unworthy of it and me. Time will ratify this conclusion one way or the other – and to Time I refer it accordingly.

Yet Harpur's last years were brightened by the devoted friendship of a poet from a younger generation, Henry Kendall. In Harpur's verse Kendall believed he was encouraging the first authentic voice of a new land, and one which uttered 'the whole truth ... before the World in all its unclouded simplicity.' Unerringly and unselfishly Kendall recognised the older man's poetic strengths, the striking originality of his achievement, and his future place as the founding figure of Australian verse.

Harpur was born at a turning-point in Australian history. In the year of his birth, 1813, the administration of Lachlan Macquarie was at its height. Under his careful governorship the colony had continued to advance from a rude penal settlement, marked by insubordination, brutal repression and crime, into a well-ordered and bustling community, circumscribed only by distance in its economic and intellectual advancement. To the west of the colony lay the virtually impenetrable Blue Mountains, to the east the vast oceans which isolated the Europeans in an unknown and inhospitable land. But in 1813 the coastal dwellers gained a sense of unlimited expansion. Blaxland, Wentworth and Lawson forged a path over the Blue Mountains, thereby rendering accessible the pastoral hinterland which Wentworth would later celebrate in terms of a promised land or 'boundless champaign . . . /Op'ning like Canaan on rapt Israel's view.' Similarly, Macquarie was encouraging a freeing of human boundaries and an escape from divisive prejudices. The blacks won his early interest and support, while he vigorously promoted the legal and social rights of the freed convict or emancipist class. These enlightened initiatives, however, met with opposition from well-to-do immigrants who sought to secure for themselves immense grazing tracts, and a rural aristocracy which claimed political pre-eminence. Macquarie struggled against these vested interests till his departure in 1822; and these groups provided Harpur with his natural enemies.

The poet's family background did much to shape his attitudes. As the son of convicts, Harpur belonged by birth as well as by inclination to the currency or native stock, who argued for social change. In his parents he had already witnessed the practices and failings engendered by the Old World's inflexible class structures. His impecunious father was condemned and transported for the theft of money, bacon and yeast, while his mother, when in her early teens, was sent to Australia in the company of hardened criminals. Moreover, their dependence on a system organised to protect the interests of a propertied and educated élite continued at Botany Bay. There Joseph and Sarah relied ultimately for their life and freedom on the goodwill of the colony's chief magnate, John Macarthur, to whom they were both assigned. Over a period of three decades, Joseph worked his way towards legal rehabilitation, economic independence, and social standing, only to see his painstaking gains wiped out in the drought year of 1829. With his father's fate before his eyes, Charles can have been under no illusion about the lot in store for a poor, uneducated and substantially friendless man like himself. He had seen the reliance of his parents on immigrant power-brokers, and in the course of his own life he would discern a repeated pattern of ruthless aggrandizement, by which the sons of the Old World assumed the new land as their due, and so deprived the locally born of their rights and of the toil of their fathers. Pelf and privilege,

Harpur would bitterly complain, counted for more than native genius, integrity and honest endeavour.

As Harpur grew to maturity, crucial issues began to emerge which would dominate colonial debate in the middle decades of the 19th century. By the close of the 1830s the foundation for most of Australia's future states had been laid, and the public was deeply divided on the many-faceted questions of education, the Aborigines, and the most desirable constitution for the colonies. For instance, should education be universally available? Should the competing religious denominations have a role in it? And did man's spiritual growth and intellectual well-being depend on factors outside their conventional purview? Generally, how you answered reflected your broader conceptions of man and society, as did your response to the country's racial tensions. The confrontation between black and white had, of course, raised moral dilemmas ever since the first European contact with the continent; but these were brought into sharp focus by the Myall massacre of 1838. There twenty-eight Aborigines, including women and children, were slain. Seven whites, in turn, were tried for murder, found guilty and hanged. The affair highlighted the problematic relationship of the blacks to European law, and the continual decimation of the Aborigines caused by expanding white settlement.

Similar questions pertained to the rights of emancipists and native-born. To the agrarian and government élites of the day, the white Australians often assumed the spectre of a rowdy, egalitarian mob, which threatened to level all class distinctions and excellences; and therefore needed the firm ruling hand of a hereditary caste, such as the squatters hoped to establish. To the democratically inclined, these pretensions to privilege were intolerable. They seemed like attempts to throttle the energies of the present generation of native-born, and to dictate the lives of successive generations through gaining control of the legislative bodies and the country's vast pastoral lands.

Nothing less than the future shape of the Australian confederation was at issue. Should the squatters hold the reins of power and form a land-based oligarchy, or should the franchise be extended to those of modest fortune? Were all men equal and capable of building society afresh; or was man irredeemably fallen and hence in need of strong guidance from above? Depending on your point of view, the continent provided evidence either of an unmitigatedly fallen state, or of the promise of continuing natural potential from which man could create a bounteous and humanized garden in the New World.

Charles Harpur's poetry and prose must be seen within the context of this ongoing debate. As he unequivocally stated, 'I am not only a democratic Republican in theory, but by every feeling of my nature. Its first principles lie fundamentally in the moral elements of my being, ready to flower and bear their proper fruit.' And his work testifies to the accuracy of this claim. Throughout his varied professional career he contributed prose pieces on most issues of contemporary interest, while his verse deals either explicity or implicity with related concerns. Most obviously, his satiric and polemical works attack current abuses and promote worthwhile goals; but even his apparently straightforward depictions of natural life reveal an essentially republican bias. Nature is consistently presented as a repository for and intermediary of Divine and lasting lore open to every man. Privileged knowledge is no longer restricted to a social or religious caste, and common man emerges as a potential legislator and self-regulator. Given this conception, moreover, the role of the poet becomes clear. He is to act the part of a prophet or seer, interpreting Providential design, admonishing backsliders, and revealing to his countrymen their spiritual heritage and national destiny. This sense of election appears most dramatically in 'The Dream by the Fountain.' There Harpur shows himself consciously choosing to be 'the Bard of thy Country' who, with his celebration of the colony as 'the cradle of Liberty,' will prepare the way for a God-ordained democracy, or, as he puts it, 'brighten the source of Australia's broad story.'

In assuming the mantle of a national prophet, Harpur was associating himself with a venerable tradition, and also acknowledging the most important literary influences on his writing. Apart from the Bible, which he read assiduously, his list of favourite authors would be headed by Milton, Shakespeare, Wordsworth and Shelley. Each of these poets, in his own fashion, attempted to direct the passions of his countrymen and to shape the future course of a nation. These attributes would have appealed to Harpur; and he frankly confessed his debt to these writers. Never slavish in his admiration, however, the Australian could advise Deniehy to study 'Wordsworth for his simple power,/Not for his namby-pamby-ness'; or praise Shelley for his pursuit of the ideal, but find fault with his superabundant imagery. Milton alone seems to have escaped serious censure. He remained for Harpur the 'Bard of Paradise', as well as the fearless defender of Divinity and republican faith. Finally, in the writings of Milton and Wordsworth, the Australian found inspiration for his own ambitious attempt to justify the creation to man, and to reveal an immanent purpose in the surrounding landscape of everyday life.

The notion of poetic mission, then, informs his writings, and is reflected in their underlying conception of human existence. Central to Harpur's vision is the belief in God's beneficent intention, although man is portrayed as having the ability to 'mar its just design.' To the poet's eye, nature offers constant indices of an 'ultimately perfect Plan.' It is evident each day in the arising sun's radiant majesty, when God re-enacts His founding creation of order from chaos, and confirms His promise that regenerative light will triumph over the forces of darkness. Similarly, it appears in each new human being who represents a birth of unspoilt Edenic innocence, a spring-time potential which, as in the beginning, may make or unmake his natural and human surrounds. Nevertheless, man's propensity to sin is not underplayed. Harpur's measured and characteristic view is summarised in 'Eden Lost,' where he asserts that stars, sun, moon, birds and beasts

> Are loyal to their mould as on
> Creation's earliest day.
>
> 'Tis Man alone – dishonest Man,
> Who schemes a plan
> Excluding brotherhood
> He only, with disnatured mind
> Becomes the Tyrant of his kind.

Here as elsewhere in his verse, culpability rests with man's mind, or 'some dread Intelligence opposed to Good.' God, by implication, is absolved of blame; the natural world is seen as still informed by the primal plan, and responsibility for the future course of a nation is shown to rest with each individual. Consequently, Harpur maintained that 'the prime object of Society is, or should be, the perfection of Man'; and all his important writings from early youth on attempt, in one form of other, to mould his country's 'thinking power.'

The works in this selection cover all periods of Harpur's production, and have been arranged to draw attention to certain major areas of his thought. Chronology has therefore been sacrificed to content, and poetry and prose are ordered in accordance with the editor's conception of what is representative, striking, or otherwise indispensable to an understanding of the poet's life and ideas. A selection of correspondence, including letters exchanged between Harpur and Kendall, constitutes the fifth section. The original spelling and punctuation of the manuscripts has been retained. No doubt some vagaries are the result of draft-composition, others of printing errors in the newspapers of the day from which Harpur culled occasional clippings. I have followed the dictates of fidelity, and attempted to give an accurate impression of the poet's text. Editorial incursions are marked in square brackets, and have been restricted to passages where Harpur's meaning might otherwise have been unclear. The Mitchell Library manuscript source of the writings in these sections is listed at the end of this book. Harpur's writings are reprinted by courtesy of the Mitchell Library, Sydney, and the La Trobe Library, State Library of Victoria; while the publication of this edition has been made possible by a generous subsidy from the Monash University Publications Committee. I also gratefully acknowledge the unflagging research assistance of Lorraine Bullock, as well as the many hours devoted to typing difficult manuscript material by Sheila Wilson and Gail Ward.

Michael Ackland
Monash University

1 • On Individual and National Destiny

Charles Harpur – His Own Epitaph

Here lies Charles Harpur, who at fifty years of age came to the conclusion, that he was living in a sham age, under a sham Government, and amongst sham friends, and that any World whatever must therefore be a better world than theirs. And having come to this conclusion, he did his dying and now lies here with one of his sons, in the hope of their meeting in some place better fitted to make them happy, and to keep them so, than this from which they have departed. And even if all that now remains of them is what remains below, – it is still well: inasmuch as in that case, they are safe from all malignity, whether proceeding from God or Devil, that would any further afflict them.

The Dream by the Fountain

Thought-weary and sad; I reclined by a Fountain
At the head of a white-cedar shaded ravine,
And the breeze that fell over the high-glooming mountain
Sang a lullaby low as I gazed-o'er the Scene.

Long I'd reclined not till slumber came o'er me,
Grateful as balm to a suffering child:
When a lofty-souled Maiden seemed standing before me
With a lyre in her hand – O so sounding and wild!

Bright was her brow, not the morning's brow brighter,
But her eyes were two midnights of passionate thought;
Light was her motion, the breeze's not lighter,
And her locks were like sunshine and shadow inwrought

Never before did my bosom inherit
Emotion so thrilling, such exquisite awe!
Never such wonder exalted my spirit
Before, as did now, through the Vision I saw.

Robed for the chase like a nymph of Diana,
Her ivory limbs were half given below –
Bare, that the pure breath of heaven might fan her,
Bare was her bosom of roseate snow.

Then lifting the lyre, and with every feeling
Sublimed as with love, she awakened the strings:
Bliss followed – and half into being came stealing
The motion and light of angelical wings.

Divine were the measures! Each voice of the wildwood
Seemed gathering head in their musical thrills –
The loud joy of streams in their strong mountain childhood,
The shouting of Echoes that look from the hills:

The moaning of trees all at midnight in motion,
When the breezes seem lost in the dark, with a rare
And sweet meaning spirit of human devotion,
All blended and woven together were there!

Ceased then the strain: and as soon as were flowing
Around but the accents that people the wild,
The Lyrist, subdued by her rapture, yet glowing,
Adjusted her mantle, approached me, and smiled:

Smiled with a look like the radiance of morning
When flushing the crystal of heaven's serene,
Blent with that darkness of beauty adorning
The world when the moon just arising is seen.

And repressing it seemed many fonder suggestions,
Calmly she spake; – I arose to my knees,
Expectantly glad, while to quiet my questions,
The wild warbled words that she uttered were these:

'I am the Muse of the evergreen Forest –
I am the spouse of thy spirit, lone Bard!
Ev'n in the days when thy boyhood thou worest,
Thy pastimes drew on thee my dearest regard.

For I felt thee, – ev'n then, wildly, wondrously musing
Of glory and grace by old Hawksbury's side,
Scenes that spread recordless round thee suffusing
With the purple of love – I beheld thee, and sighed.

Sighed – for the fire-robe of Thought had enwound thee,
Betok'ning how much that the happy most dread,
And whence there should follow, howe'er it renowned thee,
What sorrows of heart, and what labors of head!

Sighed – though thy dreams did the more but endear thee –
It seemed of the breeze, or a sigh of thine own!
I would sweep then, this lyre, gliding viewlessly near thee,
To give thy emotions, full measure and tone.

Since, have I tracked thee through dissolute places,
And saw thee with sorrow long herd with the vain;
Lured into error by false-smiling faces –
Chained by dull Fashion though scorning her chain.

Then would I prompt in the still hour of dreaming,
Some thought of thy beautiful Country again;
Of her yet to be famed streams through dark woods far gleaming –
Of her bold shores that throb to the beat of the main.

Till at last I beheld thee arise in devotion,
To shake from thy heart the vile bondage it bore,
And my joy gloried out like a morning-lit ocean,
When thy footfal I heard in the mountains once more!

Listen, rejoined one; I promise thee glory
Such as shall rise like the day-star apart,
To brighten the source of Australia's broad story,
But for this thou must give to the future thy heart!

Be then the Bard of thy Country! O rather,
Should such be thy choice than a monarchy wide!
Lo, 'tis the Land of the grave of thy father!
'Tis the cradle of Liberty! – Think, and decide.

Well hast thou chosen.' She ceased. Unreplying,
I gazed, mute with love, on her soul-moulded charms:
Deeper they glowed, her lips trembled, – and sighing
She rushed to my heart, and dissolved in my arms!*

Thus seemed she to pass – and yet something remaining,
Like a separate Soul in my soul seemed to be:
An aching delight – an extension, that paining
My spirit, yet made it more strengthy and free.

She passed – but to leave in my brain a reflection,
A fore-visioned blaze of prophetical sway;
While tones that seem gushings of mystic affection,
Flow through me by night and around me by day.

And since, or in cities or solitudes dreary,
Upon the lone hill or more lonely sea-sand,
No matter how few in my wanderings cheer me,
I know that 'tis mine 'mid the Prophets to stand!
No matter how many that blame be anear me,
I feel like a Monarch of song in the Land!

* It has been pointed out to me, that there is some resemblance between this phase of the Vision and the matter of a passage in Shelley's Alastor. But whatever of likeness there may be, my draught cannot possibly be any copy of his, for the simple but sufficient reason, that up to the time of its production, and for long after, though I may have heard of Shelley as a Poet, I had never seen a line of his writings. My acquaintance with these began as late as in '43 or '44, – namely: on the occasion of Mr Henry Parkes sending me as a present, far into the interior, a copy of Mrs Shelley's edition of them, in six volumes.

Final Note to the Miscellaneous Poems

To show under what *outre* worldly circumstances a man may yet possess, enjoy and cultivate the delights of Poesy, I will even describe mine such as they were during the composition of many of the foregoing Poems, and of all of the Notes to them. I was living alone in a sad-looking house, which, like myself, had seen better days, with but one neighbour, a Mr. Donnelly, within a mile of me, taking care of the Jerry's plains' Pound and Post Office, as agent for my brother, who was himself residing at a farm called Maryville, about three miles distant, and whom I did not see above once a week at most, and seldom so often. I had to wash, mend, bake, cook &c. for myself – the profits of my agency being only, one week with another, from five to perhaps ten shillings, or about barely enough to clothe me. I was doing nothing, and could do nothing for the future, except in the way of poetry; and its countenance therefore looked exceedingly blue upon me –

especially as I had let Fortune give me entirely the slip thitherto. Yet I was far from unhappy upon the whole; nor did I feel the solitude of my days and nights weigh so heavily as the reader might suppose. Nay, though the calls of parties on business, did not average above two per dium, the sight of their coming gave me no social pleasure, as they were persons with whom, out of the present and mechanical, I could hold little communion: and I always felt, though I might think well of them as neighbours and so forth, that my time was wasted through them, in the event of their trespassing upon it longer than was necessary for the transaction of whatever business they came upon. Such were my worldly circumstances at the time I am writing of, and yet I composed under them, I believe, many of my happiest pieces both in prose and in verse. And how fully does this result enforce the truth of Milton's lines –

> The mind is its own place, and in itself
> Can make a heaven of hell.

from Rosa or Sonnets of Love

No. IV
On First Seeing Rosa Dressed in White

Thus should she always dress! in white. To me
Such vesture seems the emblem of her mind!
Pure – spotless – innocently unconfined,
In both what chastity of style I see
Yet flowing as the breeze when it is free!
With sweet conceptions of the angelic kind,
A Virgin so arrayed, to a refined
And loving eye, doth witchingly agree.
Oh, that I were that graceful garb, infolding
All that is covetable under heaven!
Ah, me! in vain have I so strongly striven
But to admire her; for, even now, beholding
Her glowing beauty curtained thus in white,
Mine eyes are film'd with a love-thick delight!

No. XI
Rosa's Image

Her Image haunts me! Lo, I muse at even,
And straight it gathers from the gloom, to make
My soul its mirror; which (as some deep lake
Is pictured with azure smile of heaven,)
Through the hushed night retains it; when 'tis given
To take a warmer presence, and incline
A glowing cheek all blushfully to mine,
Saying – 'The heart for which thou long hast striven
With pale looks – fancy-pale, I grant thee now;
And if for pity, yet more for love's sweet sake,
My lips shall seal this promise on thy brow.'
Thus blest in sleep, who would not weep to wake,
When the cold truth from his belief must shake
Such vows, like blossoms from a shattered bough.

No. XXXIV
The Consummation

Mine after all! – my Mary! Why should I
Give to that sweet name longer a disguise?
Now that beneath the conscious seeming skies
My joy is all as open and as high!
I weep – and fondly ask the reason why?
Thinking my happy heart should otherwise
Than thus keep gushing through my happy eyes,
Now that she's mine by an enduring tie!
Mine after all – my Mary! Let the past,
With all its passionate doubt and loving sorrow,
Be nothing to me now: because at last,
Love's consummation o'er my life is cast;
Even as the sun ariseth on the morrow
Out of the dark night cloudlessly and vast.

Note to the Lass of Eulengo

I once hoped and believed that the heroine of my Song entitled as above was destined to become my Wife; but fortune was permitted to will it otherwise. I was poor, nor was she rich, and 'prudence was her o'erword aye'. I would have been content – I would have been happy to have toiled for her welfare every day of my future life, and

> The world was all before us, where to choose
> Our place of rest, and Providence our guide.

But she would not: her alledged reason for finally breaking with me, being certain imperfections in my worldly conduct. She was advised to this course by her friends. But I never pretended to be a moral saint – even to her; and the model-men, the suggested preferences, of her advisers – they, in all moral regards, were even less saintly than myself. They were, however, considerably richer.

My notions and tastes may be peculiar, but I have small patience with overmuch prudence in love, and as little relish for a cold passion as for cold soup. And what is now the fruit which *she* has gathered from these? A loveless future (supposing her love for me to have been genuine as far as it went), and a regretful – perhaps an accusing past. For the first evil, what can compensate? And secondly, if she valued me much, despite the chilling admonitions of her mere prudence (as I believe she did), there is at least so much against the self-referent wisdom of her conduct, in finally rejecting me.

I write this Note in the spirit of regret – not of complaint. Nor can she *now*, have aught to complain of. For, to be philosophical, if her prudence has been a genuine thing – a moral and not a selfish principle of conduct, the satisfaction of having thoroughly carried it out, is her proper, and should be her sufficient recompense. In acting upon it, she has been simply fulfilling, in her appointed place, her appointed duty.

But for myself,

> The wearied Bird, blown o'er the deep,
> Would sooner quit the shore,
> Than I would cross the gulf again
> That time has brought me o'er.

1847

PS (1850) The Lady-subject of the above Note was not so very prudent after all. At all events, she is at this present smiling over my shoulder as Mary Harpur: smiling magnanimously, as having just consented that the said Note, with all its faults, should ever remain wedded, even like myself, to the 'Lass of Eulengo'. To this consent, she has been moved by my most dutiful request, made in all humility, under the impression that the matter of it is very characteristic of a peculiar turn in my bygone batchelor disposition.

To the Sonnet on the Fate of Poetic Genius in a Sordid Community

This Sonnet conveys a faithful picture of my poetical fortunes at the time of its composition – and is quite as applicable to them up to the present writing. At this moment I am a wanderer and a vagabond upon the face of my native Land – after having written upon its evergreen beauty strains of feeling and imagination which, I believe, 'Men will not willingly let die'. Still, I say, 'I am a bard of no regard' in my own Australia. But my countrymen, and the world, will yet know me better. I doubt not indeed, but that I shall yet be held in honor both by them and by it: – that is, when I shall have lived down certain calumnies that are now afloat against me. One of these is, that I am a drunkard. This is mainly a lie. For though I have occasionally indulged to excess in 'strong drink', it has been only *occasionally* even during the worst periods of my life – and latterly, for a long time, I have never exceeded.* Another of these calumnies is, that I am somewhat lax in my sexual moralities. This is also mainly a lie. I have lived chastely upon the whole, throughout my entire life. Another evil belief to my prejudice in certain quarters, is, that I am somewhat atheistically given in my conversational speculations.** Now this is wholly a lie: and has been originated by incapables who did not understand me. How it could obtain in the face of even my published writings, would astonish me, did I not know from bitter experience, how ready men are to denounce as an irreligionist any and every one who may dare, in his mental intercourse with them, to travel out of some prescribed theological circle – which is, moreover, often a vitious [vicious] one.

To sum up then, had I been but half as wicked as I have been given out to be, I should, with my talents even such as they are, have had many supporters by this time; for the interests and sympathies of the bad in Australia dove-tail as it were into one another – and their name is 'legion'. As it is I have very few – the strongest proof perhaps that could be given, apart from a fashionable or fortuitous popularity, of my being upon the whole rather a good sort of man than a bad one.*** It is a proof at all events, and an emphatic one, that I have not been vitious enough to live by vice.

1848

* But men of quick temperaments must have some occasional excitement – the excitement either of love or gain or glory or *grog*; and when ever I dipped into excess, it was because I was then shut out by the cruelty of circumstances from every of the above resources but the last: becaus[e] I was utterly lonely, and hungry for sympathy, even to the eating of my own heart.

(The two following additional notes to this apologia are preserved in A92 (Ed).)

** Now this is wholly – emphatically an error; and must have arisen amongst those who did not, could not, or would not understand me. No man alive can have a firmer conviction than I have of the existence of the Deity; nor feel more assured than I do of the almighty wisdom and goodness with which [H]is providence is everlastingly operating upon the world ...

*** And – What wonder indeed is it that I should manifest, even now in my maturity, great imperfections of character? The good that is, or might have been in me, has never had fair play. For instance, of what kind have my associates been, of necessity, throughout my entire life? Men who could value nothing in me that I valued in myself: and least of all, my moral and intellectual enthusiasm. It was madness in these eyes. It was dampened therefore; oftentimes extinguished, at least for a time, during which, to my sorrow and shame, I fell to their own level – to mount again perhaps – ay[e], to mount again, but with the wings of my spirit both soiled and impaired. Still I would not greatly excuse myself nor be greatly excused. I had that within me from which better things should have proceeded: and had the world hitherto treated me with anything like justice – leaving mercy out of the question – I could now contentedly abide without a word in self-defence, the bitterest consequences of its condemnation.

To Myself, June 1855

What's the Crimean War to thee,
   Its craft and folly, blame and blunder?
Its aims are dodges plain to see,
   Its victories shams with all their thunder.

Heed not its proud but passing things –
   The royal mischiefs of their day;
But give thou Thought's immortal wings
   To glories of a purer ray:

To Freedom in her future prime,
   To Nature's everlasting lore,
To Science from her tower in Time
   Surveying the Eternal's shore.

Be such the subjects of thy thought,
   Not Old World Kings and ruling sets,
And Liberties that flounder, caught
   Like fish in diplomatic nets.

For these, if pondered, can but hurt
   The straightness of thy moral view,
And foul as with the Old World's dirt
   The virgin nature of the New.

Note to a Republican Lyric (From a Colonial Newspaper)

As I feel but little respect for Monarchy Men and Empire-worshippers (as such) I cannot apologise for speaking of them somewhat contemptuously. I am not only a democratic Republican in theory, but by every feeling of my nature. Its first principles lie rudimentally in the moral elements of my being, ready to flower forth and bear their proper fruit. Hence, as I hold myself, on the ground of God's humanity, to be politically superior to no fellow being, so, on the same ground, I can feel myself inferior to none; – that is, by privilege, or otherwise than by virtue of some appointment that has been sanctioned by a majority of my people and which appointment itself must terminate [?] at a given time. Hence too, if even the 'powers that be' are not thus sanctioned and thus determined as to time, and I submit to them, it is because I have not the power of effectual resistence, and only for so long as I lack this power.

But I will confine myself here to individualities. As I believe and affirm that no man can be noble by accident, like that of birth, or by virtue of any patent derived from a fellow mortal, so no man is ever veritably vulgar in my regard, save and except him only who is abject enough to begod a lord or a King, or who, after due enlightenment and reflection, would be himself, under any circumstances, either the one or the other. Such a man only do I esteem vulgar – and vulgar he is, whether he sit high amongst the great or herd with the rabble. Shame is upon him, and it is therefore that he cannot look upon the dignity of man in its first noble nakedness: it must be girded for him with the apron of figleaves, the sign and symbol of the Fall. It is such a man that is the veritable plebean, and it is the opposite of such a man that is the true patrician. And these must be my sentiments; – *must be*, I say, by the very mould of my nature, unless the patents both of royalty and feudal nobility can be shown to bear upon them the avouched and indisputable signature of God.

But to come down many degrees in the scale of Convention, I can admit no man to be even a gentleman who is not brave, fraternal and upright. He only who is to[o] valiant to succumb to wrong, too righteous to wink at it, and too honest to profit by it; he only can be a gentleman by the stamp and superscription of nature; and nature in this case is but the mint of God.

• NOTE TO A REPUBLICAN LYRIC •

I may be an enthusiast – I *am* an enthusiast; but I know that a grand and beautiful reason, a mighty logical necessity, is at once the cause and the sanction of my enthusiasm. And 'Right Onward' therefore, the motto of the sacred Milton, the great republican poet of England, is also *mine*.

But much may be said for the royal and aristocratical governing system of England. No doubt: but how much can be well said for it? If we are to judge of the tree by much of its fruit, the case is exceedingly ugly. For apples we are presented with the veriest crabs. For example, what a miserable ebb was the mighty and magnificent England reduced to but the other day by the most characteristic workings of this same system! After having had her most gigantic national efforts palsied and stultified by an Aberdeen and his set, she had nothing for it but to lie groaning as it were for salvation at the feet of a Palmerston or a Derby, or with the desperation of a drowner, to catch at some straw-like hope of peace derived from the death of an opposing potentate! Either must she be comforted by some titled hand or coronetted fool's head, or by some courtly accident or dodge of diplomacy, or be left to the mercy of a crisis, though at the peril of perishing. That is one slice of the most apple like looking globe in the whole growth of her governing system. And if her armies cannot conquer under the Raglans, they must be even beaten under the Raglans, for by all the sanctions of her system, are they not *their* inheritance? God help her! Were I an Englishman, and as fully conscious as I ought to be of the real magnitude of my nation, rather than be forever government ridden by such creatures as these and in a way like this, I would be a kitten and cry *mew*, or a dog and bay the moon, or even a corps battened upon by worms.

May 1855

This Southern Land of Ours

With alien hearts to frame our laws
    And cheat us as of old,
In vain our soil is rich, in vain
    'Tis seamed with virgin gold:
But the present only yields us nought,
    The future only lours
Till we dare to be a people
    In this Southern Land of Ours.

What would pygmean statesmen but
  Our new-world prospects blast,
By chaining native enterprise
  To Europe's pauper past,
With all its misery for the mass,
  And fraud-upholden powers;
But we'll yet have *men*, – like Cromwell,
  In this Southern Land of Ours.

And lo, the unploughed future, boys,
  May yet be all our own,
If hearts that love their Native Land
  Determine this alone:
To sow its years with crops of truth,
  And border these with flowers,
Till we have a *birth of heroes*
  In this Southern Land of Ours.

A Note on the Australian-born Whites from The Kangaroo Hunt

It must be confessed that there is in this part of my Poem a rather strong infusion of a *quasi* national glorification. Nevertheless there is a bright bead of truth sparkling through the spirit of it, and mantling to the surface, like an evidence of good liquor. The physical completeness of my countrymen, as a race, is undeniable; and I believe their mental and moral capacities only require adequate culture to become equally allowed and equally remarkable. A good national System of Education, by effecting this, would eventually make Australia the mother of one of the finest people in the world. And for how long shall the bigoted fears and party covetousness of irrational or dishonest sectaries be powerful enough to prevent her of this prime desideratum? Or are the soul-dwarfing and mind-distorting limitations and antagonisms of 'chartered' and unchartered priesthoods, to curse the future of Australia as they have cursed the past of Europe?

That the native born Australians are naturally capable of the highest moral and intellectual developement – that is speaking generally – is a broad fact well attested to by Phrenology; – this organic excellence being itself, to my thinking, very largely assignable to the general influences of a surpassing climate, operating conjointly with a happy admixture of races. And thoroughly advised of this great fact, I would even have my countrymen to beget in themselves a wholesome distrust of the ingrained prejudices of old-world guides and alien hirelings. For we are neither English, nor Irish, nor Scotch; – but Australians: and our career as a race should be full of boldness and invention, and as little imitative as possible. Wherefore I say again, a good System of *national* Education is our prime desideratum; and that in preparing the way for and devising the place of such a System, we must in no wise fail to be true to ourselves and to our children. We must be bravely mindful of the noble inheritance which Providence has, in this broad Australia of ours, allotted to us and to them. And finally, in devising our System of national Education, we must be full of faith in the divinity of the Spirit of Knowledge; for by a full faith of this kind shall all knowledge be ultimately eviscerated of evil. We must have also an entire belief in the religiousness of Science; for all her revelations and veritable teachings are the indubitable scriptures and precepts of God.

(I preserve the above note, because it was the first trumpet-blast that was ever blown in this country, in the cause of National Education. Afterwards too, – whenever opportunity offered, – I was amongst the first who advocated the same cause in the Journals of the day. And my reward was obloquy: for there is none more persistently (though often unconsciously) unjust, than the misbeliever in the moral needfulness of knowledge. 1860)

The Tree of Liberty
(A Song for the Future)

We'll plant the Tree of Liberty
In the centre of the Land,
And round it ranged as guardians be
A vowed and trusty band;
And sages bold and mighty-souled
Shall dress it day by day –
But woe unto the traitor who
Would break one branch away.

Then sing the Tree of Liberty
For the vow that we have made!
May it so flourish that when we
Are buried in its shade,
Fair Womanhood, and Love and Good,
All pilgrims pure, shall go
Its growth to bless for happiness –
O may it flourish so.

Till felled by gold, as Bards have told,
In the Old World once it grew,
But there its fruits were ever sold,
And only to the Few;
But here at last, whate're his caste,
Each man at nature's call,
Shall pluck as well what none may sell,
The fruit that blooms for All.

Then sing the Tree of Liberty,
And the men who shall defend
Its glorious future righteously,
For this all-righteous end:
That happiness each man to bless
Out with its growth may grow –
Our Southern Tree of Liberty
Should – *shall* ev'n flourish so!

NOTE For the republican spirit of this and others, if not all of my national poems, I can offer no apology. Why indeed, should I? believing, as I do, that men progress as sequently from monarchian to republican ideas (when they make any moral and social progress at all), as they do from feudal and despotic ones to those of a limited monarchy. This is strikingly evident in the political tendencies of all modern Colonies. Let civilised men be but placed for a few generations beyond the direct action of courtly and aristocratical influences, and the idea of Equality becomes fundamental in their sense of political and social obligation. They are republicans, in short, and mostly democrats also, before they can render a definite reason, it may be, for the 'faith that is in them.' And this results, I repeat it, from a moral and social progress purely natural to civilised men though quickened by peculiar circumstances. The empires, kingdoms, and aristocracies of Europe were founded either in military dictation, or piece-meal conquest by provincial combinations, during barbarous or semi-barbarous times, and have been perpetuated by force and craft, either despotic or legal; – by state debts and unequal Taxes (as in England), which stipend and favor the wealthy, while they grind the poor into abjectness; or by imperial war-craft and the not less imperial knout (as in Russia), which brutalise men into hordes of bloodhounds: and they neither would have originated in enlightened times, nor could have obtained over communities previously civilised, in any rational and rightly-applied sense of the term.

But though utterly a republican in my politics, speculatively, I yet believe, that it will be best for Australia to continue during the present century (at the very least) a part of the British monarchy. For even the state-botches of Downing Street are full fifty years in advance of our present half-educated wool-kings; and such forms of Government therefore, as they may from time to time fabricate for us, though upon the most threadbare models, will be altogether preferable to any things of the kind which the latter would or could tinker up in the event of a premature separation. And hence I have called the poem, parenthetically in the heading a Song for the Future. Preparatory to such an issue, we must have an entirely new set of Leading men; – men to whom sheep and wool and oxen and tallow and wages down at the zero of serfdom are not everything worthy of account in this our virgin Land of Australia; – this so sweet cradle for a new birth of Liberty.

But the mere form of a Government is, after all, a question of only secondary importance. With our prime moral and intellectual rights thoroughly – that is, constitutionally secured to us; namely, the right of all free men to pursue together, upon political and social terms of perfect equality, both their own individual happiness and their country's welfare; to discuss publicly any and every public matter; and to dissent openly from any system of Religion, or conform unmolestedly to any mode of worship, however peculiar; with these great rights thus secured, the mere official machinery of a Government were, in fact, but a progressive testing and development of the best modes of inter-municipal combination, for the general good and security of the State. And thus simplified, its places, – being conferative of onerous honor rather than of pecuniary emolument or political patronage, would no longer be gambled and scrambled for, as hitherto, by countryless lawyers and unprincipled men of talent; nor would they be convertible, as heretofore, into baits and bribes for furthering the worst designs of the self-begodding ambitionist.

1847

Finality

A heavy and desolate sense of Life
Is all the Past makes mine – and still
A cold contempt for Fortune's strife,
Despite the dread of want of bread,
Numbs, clogs, like ice, my weary will.

How little is there on the Earth
That I at length can venerate?
I see at most one world-wide dearth
Of wisdom free, true piety,
Of noble love, of honest hate.

With little hope of higher good
For Man – for *me*, of earthly bliss,
I yet withstand as I've withstood,
The evil plan man teaches man,
By valuing all things amiss.

There's nothing under the godlike Sun
Worth loving, to be bought or sold!
The only wealth by Labour won,
Besides the food supplying blood,
Is Human Excellence – not Gold!

All other things designed or done
Their only *real* value miss,
But in so far as they, each one,
And all sustain, adorn, explain,
Secure, and enter into this.

Beauty itself were nothing – no,
But for Love's golden heart and eye:
Nay, Truth were dead but for the glow
Around its shrine of minds divine –
Of martyr minds that may not die.

Why pile we stone on stone, to raise
Jail, Fane, or Public hall; – why plan
Fortress or Tower for future days;
Yet leave unbuilt, to wrong or guilt,
The nobler pile – the Mind of Man?

With *finer wool* the land to dower,
Behold how strongly we are moved!
Even while a Nation's *thinking power*,
Unvalued yet, – unnamed, we let
Grow bestial – because unimproved!

Can then the seed in God's right hand
Of happiness, when shed below,
Find fitting nurture in a Land
Of wilding soil and selfish toil?
I tell ye, Time shall answer – No!

I tell ye, that all public good,
All individual worth and peace,
All youthful nobleness of mood,
Like rose-leaves thin must wither in
The sordid breath of days like these.

O for a prophet's tongue, to teach
The truths I cannot else reveal!
O for a Conqueror's power, to reach
The holy aim that doth inflame
And nerve me with a Martyr's zeal!

'Tis vain – the sacred wish is vain!
Men but renew the strifes of old;
But value with a greed insane,
All devilish skill – all splendid ill
That fetters Truth with chains of gold!

from The True Finality

NOTE We can scarcely insist too sweepingly upon the infinite necessity there exists of a people's keeping morally up with, if not ahead of its physical progress. Such a marriage in human advancement, in so far at least as our purposes can effect it, is the only proper Finality. There is little fear of any nation (the French perhaps excepted) going ahead *too fast* in this respect. Of the Anglo Saxon races doing so, there is none. But there is constant and deadly peril of their lagging morally and intellectually too far behind their physical improvement – in which event, their material wealth is but their accumulated bane; and for which cause, I repeat it, we can scarcely keep dinning them too sweepingly with the necessity of an equal spiritual enrichment.

As for John Bull himself, as a moralist and political philosopher, – he is proverbially 'slow-bellied'. The bare idea of 'moving on' institutionally, has to be driven into his hard head as with a sledge-hammer; and the operator must still hammer away at it, to keep it there, or he will inevitably scratch it out again, in the digital dubiety of his disinclination to budge. Then another notion, – quite an ultra radical one, must be pounded into it in the same way, not to move him of itself, but simply to cause the first to fructify and grow out into act. That is, he is urged by the first, we will suppose, to go forward to meet the necessity of the times *just a rod* and no further. He doubts – argues – thinks he won't – resolves – procrastinates. By the second he is twitted with being a beef-witted laggard, and conjured to expunge the reproach forever, by dashing (that is waddling) onward a *whole mile* at a heat, like a true British lion in chase of a French donkey. This, however, 'he'll be damned if he'll do,' notwithstanding the flattering unction administered through the flourish about the lion (it being a thoroughly English one): but he will then comply, perhaps, with the requirement of the first – and advance grumblingly, *just a rod*. But not directly – not until the exact distance has been measured and remeasured, with mathematical accuracy, by two paid surveyors, the one to act as a check upon the other.

When Rosseau desiderated the savage state as the noblest for man, he was wrong. But he was led into the error by the partial perception of a great truth: namely, that the best condition for the development of the full majesty of man, were one in which the personal freedom and sovereignty of savage life should co-exist with all the artistic beneficences and moral security of civilized society. And such a condition is indeed the great end of all human community – is, Social Individualization, the Finality of the future.

And educative and social Individualization should also be infinitely more than it is, the Finality of the present: in other words, a teaching and employing process by which every individual might be improved to the full extent, and according to the specific character of his capacity. This is demanded by a new and singular (self-sustained and sustaining) order of consciousness, which is fast developing itself in the whole human race. All the great political, social, and religious interests that were originally only operant as motive powers upon men in bodies or nationally, are beginning more and more to centre and manifest themselves in Man the Individual. Centuries of thought and self-investigation – the experience for good and evil of entire races; – these, in effect, are becoming constitutionally accummulated, and additionally transmissive, in single individuals.

Hence 'the greatest good to the greatest number' *is not* a final principle of human community, and is fast giving place to another that *is*: namely, *the greatest good to each and all*. Hence too, men can be no longer the creatures of Governments: these can no longer mould them characteristically into masses; because the associative tendencies of all are beginning to cognise and perfect their end in each. Even the Austrian, — even the thinking Russian, can now grow up under the thundrous shadow of his paternal despotism, with a distinct personal consciousness of inherent independence – of the self-possession Spiritual prerogatives which reduce it, even in its apparent almightiness, to a mere temporal accident; and he can dare to look it in the face therefore, as being a Thing only, – an awful one indeed, but which, as a Person, – as a Man, he has a right to question.

And as this Individualizing process grows natively out of the Past, it cannot be arrested. It should be carried forward then; and for this to be done harmoniously, individual education upon the most liberal and adaptative scale must be speedily resorted to; so that all men, having progressed beyond the state legislation contemporaneously obtaining, may become more and more, to the destined extent, – each and all of them, Governments in themselves. This great Fact, I repeat it (to begin with the beginning of the better time coming) is the great Finality of the Future –

and should be infinitely more than it is, that of the Present as well.

But alas! it would seem that in Australia, we are still to be prevented of all efficient means for accelerating the march of knowledge, by the irrational bigotries of Sectarian Cliques. A system of general education is offered to the country, and forthwith upstarts the parson, to denounce it as improper for *his* people. The priest also, for once partially in tune with him, joins the clerical crusade, and stigmatises it as unsuitable for *his* people. For *their* people forsooth? Who made them *theirs*? Did God, think you? He did nothing of the kind. He made each and all of us for ourselves as well as for others – to choose our way, and walk singly, as individually accountable men, and not to be herded, like cattle, into blatent Sects: and until we manfully feel this to be the truth we shall continue the unthinking tools of designing badge-wearers and prejudice-mongers, who have vowed themselves, body and soul, to the separate formularies of an ignorant and illiberal past.

And all this hub-bub amongst them – this goose-cackling tempest, was occasioned by each Sect stickling for its catechism! Now an educational system that catechetically forbids doubt upon any subject, thereby precluding, or endeavouring to preclude, its future investigation on the part of the pupil, must be pernicious, because, in the first place, he should be bound in nowise to remain the child of any system, but left perfectly free to become the thinking child of man; and because, in the next place, the more all things *are investigated* the more Truth will be expressed, – it being indeed the very essence and virtue of everything real, of every thing having a primordial vitality! Error only would impose shackles upon mind. Truth is Liberty.

(The second half of the note contrasts the 'genius' of Romanism and Protestantism, respectively of communal control and individual liberty. (Ed.))

Self-Liberty

I would not be dependent, even for love,
   On man or woman. Nay, I would – I will
Be as the eagles through the heavens that move
   Boundlessly free, though separate. And as still
   A torrent, dashing from its native hill,
Doth make its own best way, be't mine to groove
My individual world-path, and approve
   Its lonely fitness with a sovereign thrill!
Thus large must be my freedom, for the need
   Is in my nature and defies dispute,
Even as a bent peculiar to its breed
   Constrains yon tree to bear its proper fruit:
   And though the pliant deem me a strange brute
What care I, being thus *myself indeed!*

Humanity

I dreamt I was a Sculptor, and had wrought
Out of a towering adamantine crag
A mighty Figure, – giant limbed, and faced
As with the front of an Homeric God.
Planted aloft upon the levelled cone
Of a vast tumulus that seemed to swell
Above the sinking outline of the view
As up from the dusk Past, – firm fixed was one
Colossal foot, the other slightly raised
As if in slow but palpable advance.

   There, in its magnitude, aloft it stood
Against the deep of heaven light flecked with clouds,
All floating motionless – but which, ere long,
On all hands reddening from the brightening east
In swift succession, though extending wide,
Did kindle, as if torch-struck, into one
Vast spreading litter of wind-tattered sheets
And shreds of golden fire; as fast the Morn,
Like the glad herald of almighty Power
Hasting in glory to create anew,
Came burning up – out of eternity.

So, towering heavenward, there aloft it stood
Full in the face of the resplendent Morn,
And I, methought, was glorying in my work.
One large arm lay upon the roomy breast,
The other held a scroll. The ample head,
Envincing in its dome-like curvatures
August though bounded majesty, was raised,
As bravely heedful o'er the brightening world
Right forth it looked with full expectant eyes,
While the drawn nostrils and the set lips showed,
Even through the gracious flexures of their mould
As they had used to smile. But on the brows
There pained a weight and weariness of thought,
And furrows spake of care. Much too of doubt
Shadowed the meaning of the mighty face;
Much was there also in its cast, that seemed
Significant of a striving to believe –
To be the leige of an ancestral Faith.
In things remote, unsecular, – more the birth
Of mystic than sciential lore, and thence
But half assured itself.

    Such was my Work:
A formal Type (though dream-designed) it seemed
Of that great ultimate of Manhood, which
By daring, hoping, doing and enduring,
Doubting, divining, – still from age to age
Doth mould the world, and lead it truthward on,
Even through its Seers, its Heroes, and its Kings:
For all who saw it were constrained, methought,
To sigh as they looked up – 'Humanity.'

2 • On Poets and Poetry •

My Own Poetry

If I might judge of the moral effect of my own Poetry upon others from its moral influence upon myself, I should opine that it will operate healthily upon the heart of my Country, and chiefly for good. I have never been so pure-minded, nor so correct in my conduct, as when in frequent communion with the spirit of its inspiration, either composing, revising, or reperusing it. Moreover, I may truly say of it, as Coleridge [h]as said of Poetry in general, that it has been to me upon the whole, *its own exceeding great reward*. And it has been such, because it has never been a mere art with me, – a tuneful medium of forced thoughts and affected passion; but always the vehicle of earnest purpose. Nay, rather might I say, that it has always been the audible expression of the inmost impulses of my moral being – the very breath of my spiritual life. And there is no purer and more sufficing joy without the pale of heaven, than that which the true poet feels, when he knows he is securing an immortal conception to his kind, by inorbing it with beauty, as with the vesture of a star.

Then considered simply as English composition, I firmly believe that these poems of mine will bear testing with no small severity. Of this I am certain, that there are no mere words in them – no big sounding phrases without meaning! I am also sure, that there are few intanglements in them of the natural order and structure of our language, [it] is seldom tossted [?] awry* by the necessiting of the metres, although those are very various and often difficult. Neither is the sense of them much intersected by the demands of the rhymes: there are positively no jerks to the right or left in any one of them for the sole purpose of circumventing a clink. Such, at least, is my judgmatical opinion, and Time will tell whether it be a correct one – time being, as an old acquaintance of mine used to say, the best almanac.

* (This phrase, which is difficult to construe, is a revision replacing the original word 'occasioned'. (Ed.))

• ON POETS AND POETRY •

Australia's First Great Poet

His lot how glorious whom the Muse shall name
   His *first* High Priest in this Arcadian clime,
And thereby clothe as with a robe of flame!
   With the creations of her Grecian prime
   Much conversant, and to like heights sublime
Lifting new matter, let him build to Fame;
Quarrying from Nature's everlasting frame
   The Parian beauty of his lofty rhyme!
Then, meetly mated, o'er his splendid page
   Shall glow his Countrywomen's lustrous eyes,
And many a future Hero's noble rage
   Find there fit nutriment; – all brave and wise
   And beautiful spirits, 'neath his native skies
Breathing his influence from age to age.

from Harpur's Lecture on Poetry

The following lecture was delivered by Mr Charles Harpur, on Thursday evening, at the School of Arts, D. H. Deniehy, Esq., in the chair.

In the following Discourse, I propose – I. To define the nature and determine the office of Poetry, and at the same time rebut certain objections as to the character of its influence. II. To show that its heaven – the ideal – is as much a part of man's nature as the sky is of the outward world; and that as man is progressive, so of course is Poetry. III. To indicate, by following out the drift of our visionary tendencies, the manner in which I conceive Poetry to be related to Prophecy. And, IV. To endeavour to explicate, in the briefest manner possible, the real, or essential difference between Poetry and Prose.

   In the recorded opinions of all men of indubitable refinement, and who were at the same time comprehensively intellectual, Poetry has ever been accounted a high and even sacred thing. Enrapturing the master spirits of all time, those of a merely mechanical order excepted, it has been crowned as it were by their united authority, with the pre-eminent style and title of the Divine Art. Nor has this empyreal distinction been unworthily accorded to an attainment, which is the art-result or 'consummate flower' of that grateful love of the beautiful, not only in its actual manifestation, but also in its conceivable possibilities, which assuredly constitutes in man affinity with the seraph. Such is Poetry as I view it, nor am I altogether singular in thus regarding it; while the poetic itself is that infinite ocean of aboriginal beauty, in the midst of which this 'divine' art is but as a painted boat, and out of which come all its virgin values. Poetry – the harmonised expression in language of an exquisite perception of the beautiful, is the territory of the poet; the Poetic – the ideal expanse in which Poetry lives and moves, is the dominion of the Muse herself.

Mere worldlings, however, and very commonplace philosophers, are ever exceedingly ready to disparage, in so far as they can, the mental values of Poetry, and to consign the influences of the Muse herself – that is to say, theoretically – to the limbo of the purely romantic, or even to pronounce them factitious by all the tests which their experience may have been able to put them to; but the more gifted children of taste are not therefore a whit the less assured, that these incorrupt possessions are amongst the most valuable legacies of the past and the truest gains of the present; and that those auroral influences live and glow in every chamber of the universe; – in all beauty and in all truth; – quickening and deepening every good thing, while the subject of raised thought, or of imaginative passion, with a more subtle spirit of delight, and a profounder reality of interest, than can ever be dreamt of by those who only converse with nature under a worldly bias, or mainly through the senses, and merely to private ends of material convenience and benefit. And it is the peculiar office of the poet, to bring these vital, but subtle, influences into the mental neighbourhood of all men; – to make them intimately felt by all. But he does not create them. It is not because he has said let them be, that they are. No; everywhere existing in the constitution of the universe, in its relation to man and thence by reflection in whatever is truly reproduced or remodelled from it by human invention, they are but ingathered, as to an attractive centre, by his sovereign imagination; not so much for self-enjoyment, as to be again given forth in immortal poetry; that is to say, condensed or sublimated, and chastened and harmonised, and made domestic and genial through the fertility of passion. And it is only after they have passed through this process, that they are perfected in the power of causing the indurated heart of the common world to soften while listening to the eloquent appeal, and at length run over with unwonted bounty – even as from the rock in Horeb, when struck by the rod of Moses, the living waters broke flooding in miraculous abundance, to become a permanent fountain in the desert, making the lonely place grateful and giving verdure to barrenness.

But I will come down in my subject on to a somewhat lower platform. Up there in the purple clouds out of which I have just dropped myself, I likened poetry in the midst of the poetic to a painted boat in the ocean of primeval beauty. But down here I will attempt to define it more after the manner of a 'man of *this* world.' It is, then, the expression in language of a fine perception of the beautiful and commanding in anything and in all things, smoothed and modulated to the satisfaction of those instincts which tend to make it an art: or it is a spirited word-painting – a representation in apt and adequate terms, and colours of thought, of what is beautiful and commanding both in persons and things; and which, in virtue of thus clothing them, reproduces the qualities it represents, and thereby subjects them more possessively to the desires of the mind than they were, or seemed to be, when only existent in their originals. Still nothing, however beautiful, is poetry of itself, or more than potentially so. To become *that*, in any final sense, it must be *characterised* by a Poet, and thereby embued with the living warmth of *his* feelings, or arrayed in the living robe of *his* imagination.

But the social bearing of poetry, as an art, is only well and worthily inclined to, when it is carried beyond this its aboriginal latitude into the service of the truthful as well as of the beautiful: Truth and Beauty being *essentially* one; nay, being one too, even in appearance, when beheld and contemplated from a sufficient height of thought. And when thus far produced, not only is poetry religious in spirit, but moral in influence.

* * *

As to the cavils of those utilitarian animals who are in the sage habit of decrying poetry as an idle un-natural art, the influence of which is to enfeeble our heads, and soften, not our hearts, but our hands and feet – their cavils, I say, are hardly worthy of grave notice, though one were but defending a rhymed treatise on kitchen gardening, or a dwarf epic in blank about Cobett's corn. That we do not live by bread alone is a saying of supreme value, for it is divinely suggestive of the fact, that the spiritual part of our nature can only be adequately sustained by a meet ethereal nourishment which is only obtainable through the ministry of the Muse; and that the full godward growth of our minds can only be derived from habitual converse with the sublime and beautiful in the laws and harmonies, and in all the seasonable changes and aspects and influences of that great constitution of things which surrounds us to infinity, and which we call the universe. And of these the true seer is the Poet, the highest interpretation, Poetry. Nor is this the whole statement; the greater includes the less. The Poet and man of taste have not only this world-range of intellectual inheritance over and above that of the mere man of utility, but they have also within them the power of knowing and enjoying quite as well as himself, every really good thing in his whole inventory of valuables. And seeing this, how should my feeling with regard to this last class of objectus, be other than one of mere wonder – that Nature, herself a poet, should have stooped to produce them – should have privileged them with life in a world so like an anthem, so filled and flowing with melody; nay, in a world so breathing and alive, as it were, and even luminous, with lyrical pre-cantations. Besides, poetry, so far from being an unnatural kind of eloquence, is the spontaneous language of an original man; and it is only after we become conventionalised, as it were, into the pistons and paddles of a worldly routine, that we descend entirely to what is called, – and well called, – plain plodding prose.

* * *

... And thus indeed should poetry work directly for Morality, though retaining intact all its self-liberty and prescriptive license, as to the manner of doing so, and the invention of its means. Nay, however fabulous in the mere letter of its construction, in the whole spirit of its influence it should work for truth as well as for beauty – and, if it do not, I say away with it! for this our planet, in the nineteenth century, should have no place for an idler even in the paths of the beautiful. For the moral ligitimation of all Poetry – of all Fable – is desirable only from this, that it causes us to love every good thing which it idealises, or whereof it treats, not only more deeply, but more wisely than before; while the effect of the same process, in regard to all things evil, should be exactly opposite – should make us dread, or hate, or despise them, not only more habitually, but in a more instructed spirit. The Poet then, who in these days, regards his art as merely amusive, is either unaware of its oracular possibilities, or he has 'fallen from his high estate', and become unequal to its destiny. He may be, upon the whole, a 'very pretty poet,' but he will do little or nothing worthy of remembrance for poetry, which should be as much the expression in its spirit of the living pressure and tendency of its age as the better prose of a newspaper. There should be nothing merely fanciful in it – nothing delusive. It should be reality idealised; raised, not mystified; for the ideal and the unreal are in nothing the same. The prosaic indeed, may incline to confound them; but the difference between them is, notwithstanding, exactly the difference between something and nothing. For whatever sanely moves us, however intangible, however viewless in itself or visionary in its import, is in a very sufficient sense *real*; and whatever does so to a salutary end, is of the nature of truth. An impalpable thought is as actual as a star, and may have as fixed a place, or an orbit as inevitable, in the spiritual world, as that has in the physical.

The moderns have too little – or rather, no faith in the ideal. Yet is it the beauteous love-birth of the mind in fruition with its empyreal affinities; a spiritual insight, however imperfect, of the yet-to-be, or of the unfulfilled. And how full of promissory evidence too, are 'these thoughts that wander through eternity,' of the Godward ascension and immortality of the soul. Yet the moderns, speaking widely, have no faith in the Ideal. With the ancients, on the contrary, Poesy and Prophecy were the same; and the deities of their mythologies were so far Realities as they were mental impersonations of the energies and efficacies of Nature. Hence they believed in their poetry. It was only a more exalted medium than their most earnest prose for the voices and types of their religion and philosophy, as well as of their joys and sorrows, their loves and wars: and the poetical disbelief of the moderns is peculiarly *modern*. It comes, however, 'by cause,' as a Polonius would say: being traceable, with the terms which indicate it 'mere poetry!' to the fact of certain ideal beliefs that were alone proper to the generations which conceived them, because strictly in keeping with their knowledge, having yet been imitatively adhered to by the poets of subsequent ones, to which they were becoming, or had become already, 'creeds outworn.'

Nevertheless, I say, there was yet enough in the poetry of the ancients to indicate, by its agreement with the ideal spirit of all succeeding time, how inherently plastic, and thence progressive in its character was the faculty that fashioned it. And upon this hint the greater moderns began to apply its resources more and more, as did Milton and Dante, to the imaginative demands of their own generations. A marked application of the faculty in these regards has signalised the present century – even to the extent of founding a school of what may be specifically called the Poetry of Progress, and for which – as expressive of its tendency and teaching – the following lines from Longfellow might be selected (with some allowance) as an appropriate motto:

> Let the dead Past bury its dead
> Act – act in the living Present;
> Heart within, and God o'erhead!

Nothing, however, of a very high order, even in its kind, has yet been achieved by the poets of this school, while the internal promise of the great mass of their productions is injured by their being outwardly marred and hunched, as it were, by the most intolerable barbarisms and defects of style. Still it may be concluded, I think, from what has been thus far said, that Poetry henceforth will more and more approve itself a meet and harmonious organ, not only for the utterance of exquisite feeling and beautiful fancy, but all manner of moral truth and social wisdom, till it again command, though on new ground, that popular belief in its divinity, which was the inspiration of the poets of Greece and the prophets of Israel.

Nor can the manner in which the poets of Greece are here associated with the seers of Israel, be held irreverent by any one, when my whole theory on this head is communicated. Whether the Jewish prophets were specially inspired by God, may be and is a question with some – but there can be no question of their having been poets. Neither can there be any, in the face of their writings, of their having been gifted with poetic genius of the very highest order – and such genius, I say, is always prophetic, always indicates by the drift of its sympathies the onward path of the gods. But, of itself, it only foretells, because it forefeels, and what it forefeels. Or, more exactly, it forefeels, or foreconceives under an idiosyncratic impressment of nature; and then *prophesies*, not by ordination or communicated privilege, but directly, by the self-force and assurance of its preconceptions, the tests of which are inherent in the possibilities of our destiny. Ideality is the very organ of spiritual progress, and great poets, possessing this pre-eminently, and speaking at large through its Sybiline instinct, but fore-characterise in the divine tone of their beatitudes, and forecast in the exalted beauty of their impersonations and of the conditions surrounding them, that reunion with Paradise – with the perfect – which it promises to the future. Still the bitter memories of the past and the grim realities of the present – their envyings, their faithlessness, their bigotry – are forever warningly hanging over and vengefully darkening around them; and they are thus constrained, as it were, to forebode as well the fact of some crowning martyrdom, as at once a necessary acme to the malignity of evil, and a Promethean signal of the beginning of the better time – the era of regeneration. The predicted Redeemer must be a man of sorrows and acquainted with grief; must for truth's sake submit to indignities manifold, and even to death; – but only to have victory over hell and the grave – victory for all, by the almightiness of love. And forasmuch as death is still in the world, is not such a victory asked for from the bottom of all hearts? Yes. But in the great heart of the poet the divine certainty of it is also forefelt, and thence ascending into his ideal faculty, becomes there fore-visioned in the manner I have supposed, or in some other more or less agreeing with it – and is then harped forth to the listening hope of the world in the very rapture of prophecy.

Bible Poetry and Piety

I am (and always have been) a great reader of the Bible, of the Psalms especially, which I admire above all its other contents (except the Book of Job) both for their piety and their poetry. And it is my opinion, that whoever will read them thoughtfully, will also admire them on both these accounts; not so greatly as I do perhaps, but greatly. For though they exhibit upon the whole, a great harping on the same string, and consequently, much want of invention, I know of no other compositions in which there are finer occasional forms of imaginative emotion, or in which the moral sentiment for the most part is more nobly humane and exaltedly pious. Of course, I am leaving their special divinity out of view – leaving it to theologians. But, for example, what a world of *desiring* (and, I would hope, *prophetic*) benevolence is skied over by the measureless fraternity of a single couplet like the following:

> The needy shall not always be forgotten:
> The expectation of the poor shall not perish forever.

Then, if we consider them religiously, they are quick throughout with passages like the ensuing; from which a very perfection of God-dependence comes instant and breathing, as from the heart of some living creature made immortal by faith: and in which there are conceptions of the eternity of Providence so large-looming and stable, that they may be adequately imaged by nothing earthly – not even by the apparently unshakeable mountains.

Thy righteousness is *like the great mountains*; thy judgments are a *great deep*: thou possessest both man and beast. How excellent is thy loving kindness: O God! therefore the childen of men *put their trust under the shadow of thy wings*. They shall be abundantly satisfied with the fatness of thy house; and thou shalt make them *to drink of the river of thy pleasures. For with Thee is the fountain of life.*

Less sublime, but equally beautiful in the primaeval view of its poetry, is the passage below. With the rime of nearly three thousand years encrusting its expression, it is yet the mirror of a picture that is fresh and new, and everywhere alive, and so will it be forever: for it is glad and green as it were with the youthhood of Time. It deals with Nature as with some out-of-door Divinity, keeping herself aloof from whatever is sophisticate. Hence, there are no urban intimations in it – no toiling crowds – no premonitions of the din and dust of Trade. But all its images and occupations are simple and healthgiving, with the morning spirit of the Foreworld lying broad over them. And let our Political Economy urge what it will, in all this, there is somewhat very taking to the imagination and somewhat too, which primordially agrees with it.

Thou crownest the year with thy goodness, and thy paths drop fatness. They drop on the pastures of the wilderness: and *the little hills rejoice on every side*: the pastures are *clothed with flocks*; the valleys are covered over with corn: they *shout* for joy; they also *sing*.

How unflinchingly expressive of spiritual trust is the passage following:

God is our refuge and strength, a very present help in trouble. Therefore will not *we* fear, though the earth be removed, and though the mountains be carried into the midst of the sea.

The natural piety and God-dependence of passages like these, can only be exceeded (if exceeded at all) by some things in Job: such as, for example:

The blessing of him that was ready to perish came upon me: and I caused *the widow's heart to sing for joy*. I put on righteousness, and *it clothed me*: my judgment was as a robe and diadem. I was *eyes to the blind*, and *feet* was I *to the lame*. I was a *father to the poor*: And the cause that I knew not I searched out.

This is certainly as perfect a summary of the social part of pure and undefiled religion as ever was written. Amplify it, and you weaken it: take anything away from it, and you deform it; for it is a perfect sphere. Then for the expression of an utter spiritual resignation to the will of God, see what follows:

Naked came I out of my mother's womb, and naked shall I return thither: the Lord *gave*, and the Lord hath *taken away; blessed be the name of the Lord*.

And finally:

Though He *slay* me, yet will I *trust* in Him.

Talent and Genius

Accuracy of perception backed by sound judgment is Talent: add a profound imagination, and it is Genius. Genius includes Talent. It is a superstructure upon it: or, to speak mathematically, it is Talent *produced*. But by no process of Art is Talent thus produceable: it is the work of a primal energy. The aboriginal stuff of both lies bedded in nature, under inevitable limits: and culture can do no more than temper the substance, and smooth away all sharpness from its natural demarkations. And even though it should be able so far to efface these natural lines of distinction, as to lose them to the eye of common observation, still are they there, graining inward and through the entire block, fixed and inexpungable as the hand writing of Fate.

Tact is not at all touched upon in the above discrimination, because it is an essential constituent of neither Talent nor Genius, and may be absent from both. It is of the self-regarding instincts, not of the intellect, and wholly time serving. Wherefore, perhaps, both Talent and Genius without it, are eventually the better for its absence: for it is merely the application of them, and chiefly by suppressions of their energy, to present, partial, and selfish ends.

Wordsworth's Poetry

How much, O Wordsworth! in this world how much
   Has thy surpassing lore made rich for me,
   Of what was once unprized. A nameless tree –
A wilding flower – the merest hues that touch
The common clouds – lit summits – verdant leas –
   With every woodland murmur, every song
   Of bird or brook, as heard to gush along
In each fresh on-'scape of some bough caught breeze,
Have thence a charm to thrill my bosom's core,
   And gift me with a vast capacity
For innocent joy: such as was mine before
   Not even in boyhood, and that comes thus free
From things on all hands *now*, because they store
   Some inspiration of thy Poetry.

Early and Late Art

   When Art is young, it slighteth Nature;
   When old, it loves her every feature.

NOTE Look at yon savage's nulla-nulla. It is a sapling plucked up by the roots, and with the tap-block rounded into a club. Infinite labor must it have cost its primitive maker so to fashion it, with such tools as he had; and yet the curious and beautiful foldings and involutions of the tap-block, as it writhed and lessened upward into the bole, are all smoothed clean away, in accordance with an evident desire on the part of its barbarian fashioner, to displace as much of nature as possible, by such rude art as he was master of. In the same spirit, the old Egyptians excluded in their statuary all appearance of motion, which, by making it easily life-like, would have concealed, in effect, the ostentatious labor of Art. So thought the rude artist – or so he felt, instinctively. And so is it ever with Art in its infancy. It has no faith in Nature, but rather suspects her of being a bungler. Hence it would annul, in order to remodel her creations, and be as much as possible alone, – distorting, or making tasteless, whatever it touches. In its progress towards perfection, however, it acquires a truer insight, and acts upon a contrary endeavour. It then aims at the displacement, or obliteration, of no evidence of Nature, which may in anywise co-exist with its own essential demands.

Review of a poem by Kendall

This November number opens with a poem by Mr. Henry Kendall, in which tor[r]ents *moan* (though after a somewhat *roaring* fashion no doubt), shades are *dreamy* (as if someone is taking a nap in them), suns *slumbrous* (having to journey so persistently in all weathers and seasons), noons *burn mute* (consuming their own smoke), &c. &c., with that fatal alacrity which all such matters attain to, when in his hands. And why the particular moss-region alluded to in the poem, as lying amid *somnolent* stones, should be wholly free to 'soft October', and not to 'fierce December' as well is a question transcending all our critical acumen. Then why is 'Autumn like a gipsy bold'? And most certain we are, that a gipsy is not much given to 'gathering grapes and *grain*', though he may be always very readily disposed to appropriate them after they have been gathered by others. Nor is the Poet definite enough. After telling us that he and his fair friend were in the habit of sucking peaches and plums, while making a couch of the moss, he should have added, if only for the grace of giving a manipulative sort of finish to the manner of this habit, that they always threw away both the skins and the stones. But the vital defect of the piece is the nothingness of its subject; which indeed, is so inferior to the treatment, that even it is thereby degraded; – a critical result inevitable, whenever a disparity of this sort becomes immediately obvious.

To Twank*

Ah! Daniel mine, some Muse malign
   Hath skimm'd thy judgements cream away
But take a slice of 'good advice' –
   Even *that* I proffer thee today.

Again read Shakespear by the hour, –
   Read Milton more – McDonald less –
And Wordsworth for his simple power,
   Not for his namby-pamby-ness.

* (Twank – name under which Daniel Deniehy appeared in his satirical piece *How I became Attorney-General of New Barataria* (Ed.))

And know, – 'twere better to esteem
    What's best in Byron's godless 'Don'
Than with crude Browning much to dream,
    Or wire-draw through with Tennyson.

And better at the 'woes of Moore'
    To shed the artificial tear,
Than doat with eunuch passion o'er
    The *feeble* beauties of De Vere.

Modern Poetry

How I hate those modern Poems
    Vaguer, looser than a dream!
Pointless things that look like proems
    Only, to some held-back theme!
Wild unequal, agitated,
As by steam ill-regulated –
    Balder-dashie steam!
And if (in fine) not super-lyrical,
Then vapid, almost to a miracle.

from The Nevers of Poetry

Never say aught in Verse, or grave or gay,
That you in Prose would hesitate to say;
Or let your head in lofty numbers tell
What your heart deems but fit for doggerel.

from Finish of Style

A last fine touch will add to, not diminish
The value of all beauty – never doubt it;
And what deserveth not a perfect finish,
Must, even so, be doubly bad without it.

The Perfect Poet

The animal force and feeling of Byron, with the mental sensuousness of Keats, the moral depth of Wordsworth, and the gorgeous ideality of Shelley, in equal proportions and intimately blended in the constitution of one man, would make *him*, perhaps, a perfect Poet. I say, *perhaps*; – for it would still be questionable whether a perfect Poet were a possible character. And it would also be questionable, whether it should be a desirable one; for, as judged from below, or out of its own consummate sphere (and by spirits not equally free of that sphere, absolutely or potentially), its very roundness would preclude all typic affinity and appreciable raciness: and partly from this cause, and partly from sheer elevation, the 'fit audiance' would indeed be 'few', if not altogether wanting. His poems would not tell: they would not hit hard enough upon the coarse materials constituting the current public. All the salient points and angles of a general sympathy with an imperfect race would be rounded away from them by the perfection of their author. In a word, they would be a cloth of gold that would not cut into common wear, and would never for that reason come into popular appliance: for the human can only heartily appreciate the human – not the angelic.

Andrew Marvell

Though as poor a gentleman, perhaps, as there then was in all England, Marvell's undoubted patriotism maintained for him an unshaken seat in the Parliaments of his country, and that, too, in the reign of one of its most unprincipled monarchs. This is a glorious fact. And it is honorable to be able to say of human nature, even in its worst times and places, that men, whose public honesty is known and indisputable, have always a commanding popular influence. The reason is this, and let us be proud of it: – We have an instinctive trust in the wisdom of moral rectitude. We feel that to think and act righteously in most cases, we have but to think and act faithfully in all.

And Marvell was gloriously incorruptible; in which fact resided the secret of his so firm hold upon a constituency that seems to have been worthy of him. It was a fact, however, which that royal miscreant, the second Charles, naturally persisted in doubting, until he had it subjected to the test of a large sum of money. I am aware that the authenticity of the story of Marvell's treating with a quiet, matter of course, and therefore magnanimous contempt, both the Lord Chancellor, and his vile master's thousand pound bribe, has been discredited in some quarters. But for myself, I can heartily believe it notwithstanding. Such a course of conduct was all but inevitable in a bosom friend and companion of Milton. Nay, however marvellous it may appear in the eyes of modern politicians, I can freely accept the fact of this being only and merely MARVELLISH.

Of course he was a Commonwealth man in heart and soul to the last. Republicanism, indeed, in some form, is the political, or rather fraternal element with which spirits of his order, – at once simple and consciously majestic, – have a native relationship – an affinity, in short, amounting very often to an absolute idiosyncracy. They desire not, in their great singleness of heart, to be any man's lord and master; and are at the same time conscious, in the true sovereignty of their intellect, that they are properly inferior to none. Great Poets and Genuine lovers of great poetry are always democratic or popular in the inner spirit of their character; and the reason is obvious enough under adequate observation. Their universality of sympathy – that order of temperament in fact, which constitutes the highest poetical genius and the finest poetical taste, naturally allies them to the interests of the many, rather than to those of the few, because the first kind are of nature and humanity, while the last are merely or mostly of convention and class. 'One touch of nature,' says Shakespeare, 'makes the whole world kin!' how much more so then, to the fraternal apprehension of a great poet, the thousand natural touches, and fulfilling sympathies, and anti conventional concords, which make up, and give roundness and original freedom to the large type of his humanity, and which are the born secrets and sanctions of his power over the spirit of his race, not for an age or a century merely, but for all generations and for all time.

But were Homer and Shakespeare thus popular in their inner natures? They were; in so far, at least, as they were anything politically. Their sympathetic largeness of heart necessarily implies as much; and the democratic spirit is not specifically envinced in their writings, because, being dramatic narrators (both of them) they dealt only in such humanities as were already to be found, and in these, too, as already circumstanced, and not as they would have conceived or placed them for themselves, in 'bodying forth' the desirable. As it is, whenever they do travel beyond their vocational limits of incident and character, and speak out of themselves, the sentiments of both are strikingly popular; – enough so to verify, as far as they go, the preceding theory.

But to return to Marvell. Not only was he a great lover of great poetry; he was also himself a poet of no mean order. And there is much to show that the pure, patriotic spirits amongst the moderns, those of a merely mechanical order excepted, were first impassioned for public virtue by the persuasive breath of Poesie, as in their glowing spring time it met them, warmed and vitalised, as it were with all the best worth valour of the past; and that their noblest designs were greatly nourished afterwards, and kept fervent by the enthusiastic eulogies of contemporary poets. But it is only poetry of the highest order – poetry that is very wisdom of right feeling and legitimate passion, that can be thus influential towards the public exaltation of naturally noble and capable intellects.

To the Criticlings of Doggreldom

There are select Spirits for whom it is ordained that their fame shall be in the world an existence like that of Virtue, which owes its being to the struggles it makes, and its vigor to the enemies whom it provokes.

Wordsworth

> Dogs or men! – for I flatter you in saying
> That ye are dogs, your betters far.

Byron

Why howl ye at my star? It dooms you all!
   Why was the Galilean's light maligned
Of old, by all blind leaders of the blind?
His rising prophesied *their* final fall!
– I pour forth honey, and with tongues of gall
   Ye lap it! This my Country's common wind
Have I made lyrical – and lo, *your kind*
   All therefore hate me, and the effect miscall!
But always, when an eagle with strong wings
   Comes sweeping o'er yon wood, a rabble flight
Of chattering pies send up their jargonings,
   And hustle round him in ludicrous spite,
   While he himself, in his majestic might,
Moves on, unhindered by the paltry things!

Poetical Egotism

NOTE The egotism of Poets is proverbial. It is moreover generally considered quite as proper to them as any other part of their style; because, it is likely, that but for this openness of self reference, the Edens of their creative imaginations would remain forever locked against the vulgar gaze of the world. Looking then upon this very egotism as the primary bias to that inward research which forbids a Milton or a Shelley, by the discovered and discoverable riches of their secret souls, from concenting to a 'mute, inglorious' fellowship with the common oblivion of the grave – looking upon it, I would say, as a sort of Open Sesame, or pronounial key to these, who would wish that it should ever become rusted, when in meet hands, and for lack of constant use? 'Nobody that I consider anybody!' respondeth the poetical reader: and upon this hint, I will even, at this present, take a dip into the various ways in which this quality of feeling looks through the lives and writings of such of our Poets as I have just now in reading.

To begin with, then, with the greatest: in Shakspear /who is ignorantly supposed to have been devoid of it/ it has all the lustiness of an English May morning, that 'puts a spirit of youth in everything.' /See his Sonnets./ With what a palpable relish too, does he slip 'my lines' into the mouth of Hamlet in his advice to the Players? And there it is like a judicious smack of the lips after a hearty though passing pull at a 'beaker full of the warm South.' In Waller it is redolent of a well-scented beau, 'who wrote with ease', and sweetened his leisure with being exceedingly Saccharissa-loving. In Dryden it is scholarly, with, at the same time, a shrewdly mercantile cast in its complexion. 'I am satisfied there is no person who can *do* /translate/ the things you require better than I'. /See his letters to the Booksellers./ In the courtly Addison, I hardly know how to describe the manner of it. It never comes out very obviously; and yet, being Pa's own darling, we may constantly detect in a kind of bo-peep rebellion against his well-bred arrangements for confining it to the literary nursery. In *wee* Pope it is nice even to squeamishness, and remarkably *partial* to a grotto that happened to be its master's; being as exclusively literary withal as the famous Mary Montigue's bluest pair of stockings. In Burns, how wilfully is it wont to display itself through an impolitic affectation of the very rusticity from under which, in his youth, he had so ambitiously struggled – as though it should say, 'In the honest presence of Nature's gentleman, a fig for the mere gentility of the world!' In Moore it is a sort of sentimental dandyism, bathing itself in Castaly, for the *eclat* of doing so, and from an amorous admiration of the fancy-pictured *personal* charms of the Muses. In the Lord Byron it often mounts up into something that is exceedingly fine; especially when his proper manhood stands proudly apart from his accidental lordship: but it degenerates as often – more often – into littleness. In Leigh Hunt it is the very confidence of an amiable sincerity, like the outspoken frankness of a good woman; fresh and bounding too as a wave, and sunny as the longest day of Summer. In Shelley it is charity, repulsed and bleeding, and diving for solace into the lovely mystery of itself. In Wordsworth it is the surging over of a mighty intellectual consciousness, disturbed by the disparaging clamours of contemporary incapables. But of all intellectual egotists Milton is the noblest. Every feeling within us that is lofty and lasting, responds to his magnificent self-valuations as to the resounding tones of a trumpet. They invite us heavenward, like the mystical steps of Jacob's ladder, illumined with the glory of ascending angels. However reaching, there is no apparent presumption in them; however unqualified, nothing offensive. For we feel, through the medium of all that is least mortal in ourselves, that they result natively from a surpassing spiritual consciousness! – that they are founded on a rational conviction of indestructible intellectuality as upon a rock of ages.

The scene I had in mind, while musing this 'Dream by the Fountain', is a ravine amongst the mountains south of Jerry's Plains,* at the head of which there is a constant supply of delicious spring water, in a natural tank welled by Time in the solid face of a large flat-lying rock.

* Aboriginally, *Pullinymberi*

from Harpur's Lecture on Poetry

But to indulge for a moment in a more fanciful view of our subject. The creations of poetry may be said to stand in such relation to ordinary life, as dreams do to the condition of slumber. When the tone of this state is healthy, these are cheerful, full of promise, beautifully fantastic. When diseased, on the other hand, they are ugly boding, full of horror, monstrously incongrous. So is it, speaking broadly, with the creations of poetry, according as the individual minds in which they are produced, and the social soil on which they are intended to operate, are morally healthy or otherwise. And, to continue the analogy in the better part of its agreement, her winged things of love are also, in their forward flight – like dreams, or what we may suppose of dreams – sometimes prophetic. Like these, too, in a salubrious sphere, they beautify the common; nay, they transmute deformity into loveliness, and the terrible into the attractive. They annihilate distance, as with the 'wings of the morning,' and set captivity at large, as by unchainable memories of the breezy liberties of the mountains. In fine, they recall the past, enchant the present, and realise the future – restore the lost, renew the changed, enrich the poor, and reunite by an immortalising picture-power, the living and the dead. And upon the merits of this analogy, fanciful as it may be, I venture to affirm that a society which has no high place for poetry, like a mind that is not lively enough to dream well, is worse than rude, and almost worse than bad, for it is most miserably dull.

• ON POETS AND POETRY •
The Tower of the Dream

Part I

How wonderful are Dreams! Yet, are they but
(As some suppose) the thin disjoining shades
Of facts or feelings long foregone or late,
As recomposed and put in ghostly act,
And strange procession, wildly mixed, and yet
So life-like, though thus composite and wild,
By mimic Fancy; when, alone awake,
And thence unhindered in her mystic craft,
She tracks again the drifts of wearied Thought,
Itself sunk sleepward! Wonderful no less
Are they though this be true; and wondrous more
Is she who in the dark, and stript of sense,
Can claim such sovereignty – the Queen of Art!
For what a cunning painter is she then,
Who hurriedly embodying from the waste
Of things memorial littering life's dim floor,
The forms and features, manifold and quaint,
That crowd the timeless vistas of a Dream,
Fails never in a stroke; and breathes as well
(With powers that laugh at Sculpture, – or make good
The fabled influence of Pygmalion's weird
Devotion to his own creative craft)
A spirit of motion into all her work –
The test of Deity; – inspiring too
Her phantom creatures with more eloquent tones
Than ever broke in subtle light-like waves
Upon the province of a waking ear.

But are they more? Sure glimpses oft, though vague,
Derived from some unnavigable Sea
Of mystic being, on whose lonely shore
The normal terminates; and where the pent,
Impatient Soul, from its sleep-shrouded crib,
Is sometimes wont to slip, and roam at large,
Like Crusoe, staring forth; or musing stand
As did the intelligence of Newton once
On the bare beach of Time, while the great deep
Of Truth, by Science yet uncharted, loomed
In shoreless width, – illimitably out,
Under the incommunicable sky?

No answer cometh, and as vain is all
Conjecture: they are Dreams! but wonderful,
However we may rank them in our lore.
And worthy of some fond record are those states
Of our interior being, though aberrant,
That with so capable a wand can bring
Back to the faded heart, the rosy flush
And sweetness of a long fled love, or touch
The eyes of an old enmity with tears
Of a yet older friendship; or restore
A world-lost mate, or reunite in joy
The living and the dead! And this can Dreams:
With more as wonderful; – can, when so wills
Their wands weird wielder, whatsoe'er it be,
Lift up the fallen – fallen however low!
Rejuvenate the worn, enrich the poor,
The past imparadise, and enchant the present;
Build in the future higher than the hope
Of Power, when boldest, ever dared to soar;
Annul, as with the sanction of the Infinite,
The prison bars of place, the dens of time, –
Giving the rigid and cold clanking chain
Which Force, that grey iniquity, hath clenched
About its captive, to relent, – yea, stretch
Forth into Fairy Land; or melt like wax
In that fierce life whose spirit lightens wide
Round Freedom, seated on his mountain throne!
Or witching Memory, where she darkling lies,
Can so accomplish her that she can make
All brute bulk ocular – the great Earth itself
Diaphanous, like a mighty globe of glass
Hung in the dim Inane, and thence reveal
Some yearned-for hearth at the antipodes,
With all its loves; or spread at once her wings
O'er all the eras of a wandering life,
As from the orient to the ends of heaven
The silvery fans of light, evolving, show
All things beneath them in one world-wide act,
Instant and universal. – Wonderful!

But not thus always are our dreams benign:
Oft are they miscreations – gloomier worlds,
Crowded tempestuously with Wrongs and Fears,
More ghastly than the Actual ever knew;
And rent with racking noises – such as might,
If audible ever to a soul awake,
Go thundering only through the wastes of Hell.

So wonderful are Dreams: and I have known
Many most wild and strange. And once, long since,
As in the death-like mystery of Sleep
My body lay impalled, my soul arose
And journeyed outward in a Dream of Wonder,
In the mid hour of a dark night, methought
I roamed the margin of a waveless Lake,
That, in the knotted forehead of the land
Deep sunken, like a huge Cyclopean eye,
Lidless and void of speculation, stared
Glassily up, – forever sleepless, – up
At the wide vault of heaven; and that I had
Also a vague and mystic consciousness
That over against me, on the farther shore,
Which yet I might not see, there stood a Tower
Such as we read of in some old romance.

The darkness darkened, until overhead
Solidly black the starless heaven domed,
And earth was one wide blot; – when, as I looked,
A light swung blazing from the tower (as yet
Prophesied only in imagination,)
And brought at once its rounded structure forth
Out of the mighty gloom, wherein till then
So shut was its tall presence, that it seemed
As therewith one in visual consistence.
And when this light had steadied, hanging there
Suspended as by magic, I might see
In the wide lake, whose whole disc, now first shown,
Glimmered enormous, – the far falling stream
Of its wild radiance, columnar and vast,
Reach quivering – down, like a great shaft of fire,
Through the lit fluid, that, so lightened, seemed
A vague abysm infinitely deep.

Long at that wild light was I gazing held
In speechless wonder – till I thence could feel
A strange and thrillingly attractive power
In gradual operation; and ere long
My bodily weight seemed witched away, and up
I mounted, poised within the passive air;
Then glode ascendingly sheer o'er the lake,
Which far below, as tow'rds the wondrous light
The attraction drew me, I beheld illumined
Even to its sullen depths with shifting beams,
That tangled Tower-ward into one broad path
Of multifarious splendour – *one* red blaze
Yet various, interwrithing, wild and quick,
As every molecule of the watery mass
Had an organic life, and played a part
Restlessly proper to its wayward self,
Though tending all into one glow of bright
Disunion in bright union – *one* red blaze.

   Still poised within the soft air, on I slid:
Nor knew I why – but my amaze wore off
As thus I glode over the lake, and still
Approached the Tower, and that so wondrous light!
And soon, instead, a many-branching warmth
Like the sweet inklings of new love, began
To tingle in my blood, and so divine
The nearness of some yet unseen Content,
Still nearing, or some yet inaudible Joy,
So great, so reconciling, that it seemed
It was a golden destiny whose spell
Had lifted me aloft, and Tower-ward on
Thus richly attracted: – and with this so sweet
Conception – lo, how beautiful a change!

Part II

Within a circular balcony, whose roof
Was fluted silver, ledging at the eaves
Outward, and resting upon shafts of jet,
Whose polished pencils, in a curving row,
Descending to an ivory balustrade,
Glistened in contrast with a covert gleam;
And which, high up the Tower, emporched a huge
And brazen door – behold a Lady, all
Of light immaculate! Yea, face and form

All of a Hesper radiancy composed,
And lovelier than lustrous, stood alone,
Yet, as it seemed, expectant; for as still
She witched me tow'rds her, she kept beckoning still
With tiny hand more splendid than a star:
Beckoning and smiling – not as mortals smile,
With visible throes, to the mere face confined,
But with her whole bright influence all at once
In gracious act – as the Immortals smile,
God-happy; or as smiles the morning, when
Its subtle lips in rosy glory part
And redden lengthwise, under and above
Full many a pearly cloud, and breathe the while
A golden prevalence of power abroad,
That taketh all the orient heaven and earth
Into the glory of its own delight –
Transfiguring both! And with a voice intense
And intimately tender as the first
Fine feeling of a love-born bliss – and oh!
More silvery in its sweetness to the soul's
Oracular ear, than seemeth to the eye
The wild white radiance of the maiden Moon,
When from some cape's dark beak her rising mass
Looks o'er the ocean – even with such a voice,
So keen, so silvery, did she ask me then,
'Where hast thou stayed so long? Oh, tell me where!'

   With thrilling ears and heart, I heard – but felt
Pass from me forth a cry of sudden fear,
As swooning through the wildness of my joy,
Methought I drifted: – whither? All was now
One wide cold blank – the Lady and the Tower –
The gleaming Lake, with all around it – one
Wide dreary blank, – the drearier for that still
A dizzy, clinging, ghostly consciousness
Kept flickering from mine inmost pulse of life,
Like a far meteor in some dismal marsh:
How long I dreamt not – but the thrilling warmth
That like the new birth of a passionate bliss,
Erewhile had searched me to the quick, again
Shuddered within me, – more and more, – until
Mine eyes had opened under *two* that made
All else like darkness; and upon my cheek
A breath that seemed the final spirit of health

And floral sweetness, harbingered once more
The fond enquiry of that silver voice
Which once to have heard was never to forget –
'Where hast thou stayed so long? Oh, tell me where!'

And when she thus in her so wondrous way
Had spoken, there came warbled as it seemed
In mystical respondence to her voice,
Still music, such as Eolus gives forth,
But purer, deeper; – warbled as from some
Unsearchable recess of soul supreme –
Some depth of the Eternal echoing thence
Through the sweet meanings of its spirit speech,
The fond enquiry that awoke me now:
'Where hast thou stayed so long? Oh, tell me where!'

I answered not, but followed, in mute love
The beamy glances of her eyes with mine,
As in that balcony which up the Tower
Emporched the brazen door, methought I now
Close at her side reclined upon a couch
Of purple, blazoned all with stars of gold,
Tremblingly rayed with spiculated gems, –
And argent moons, – and bearing cushions, rough
(Save where they met the flexure of the arm)
With sheaves of flowers in glowing tissue wrought.
Thus sat we, looking forth; nor did I marvel,
As her's now led my vision, to remark
How the broad Lake, with its green shelving shores,
Swarming with honey-yielding flowers, or hung
With vines in masses, bunched with fruit; and thence
The prospect all – hills, skies, and winding vales,
And bloomy forests of unspeakable beauty,
Were basking in the blessedness of a day
So goldenly serene, that never yet
The perfect power of life-essential light
Might so enrobe, since Paradise was lost,
The common world inhabited by man.

I saw all this surpassing beauty – but
I saw it thus through her superior life,
As orbing mine in love – yea, saw it through
Her mystic moon-like sphere of being, that seemed
(Transpicuously) the inexhaustible source
Of holiest motives, and truth-breathing thoughts –

Breathing abroad like odours from a flower;
And orient idealities; and more
Of rosy passion, and affectionate joy, –
And earnest tenderness, that many souls
Of earth's most fervent and ecstatic daughters
United might possess; all interflowing
Through the fine issues of a love at once
Wilful and nice, but sanctioned none the less
By its so brilliant purity. Nor might
The glassy Lake below more quickly give
Nimble impressions of the coming wind's
Invisible footsteps, dimpling swift along,
Than instant tokens of communion sweet
With outward beauty's subtle spirit, passed
Forth from her eyes, and thence in lambent waves
Suffused and lightened o'er the splendid whole
Of her bright visage, or about her head
In spheres ran raying like a glory of bliss!

   But as upon the wonder of her beauty
My soul now feasted, even till it seemed
Instinct with kindred lustre, – lo, her eyes
Suddenly saddened; then abstractedly
Outfixing them as on some far wild thought
That darkened up like a portentous cloud,
Over the morning of our peace, she flung
Her silver voice into a mystic song
Of many measures, which as forth they went,
Slid all into a sweet abundant flood
Of metric melody! And with this, as still
She poured it out, invisible Singers mixed
A choral burden that prolonged the strain's
Rich concords, till the echoes of the hills
Came challengingly forth, and backward then
Subsiding like a refluent wave, afar,
Blent all into *one* mystery of sound –
One manifold cadence – dying down. The Song
(Which strangely seemed through all its mystic drift
Addressed to the so stubborn fact, that I
Was sleeping, and its utterer but a Dream)
Is traced upon the tablet of my soul
In shining lines that intonate themselves –
Not sounding to the ear, but to the thought,
Out of the vague vast of the Wonderful!

And might when hardened into mortal speech,
And narrowed from its wide and various sweep
Into such flows as make our waking rhymes
Most wildly musical, be written thus:

The Song

   Wide apart – wide apart,
    In old Time's dim heart
One terrible Fiend doth his stern watch keep
    Over the mystery
      Lovely and deep,
    Locked up in thy history,
      Beautiful Sleep!

   Could we disarm him –
   Could we but charm him
The soul of the sleeper might happily leap
Through the darkness so deathly and deep
    That shroudeth the triple divinity
    Composing thy mystical Trinity:
      Liberty, Gratitude,
      Boundless Beatitude,
    Beautiful Spirit of Sleep!

   Beautiful Spirit of Sleep!
   Could we confound him
    Who darkens thy throne –
   Could we surround him
    With spells like thy own;
      For the divinity
      Then of thy Trinity,
   Oh, what a blesseder reign were begun!
   For then were it evermore *one*
With all that soul, freed from the body's strait scheme,
Inherits of seer-light and mystical dream!

   And to sleep were to die
    Into life in the Infinite,
   Holy and high,
    Spotless and bright,
   And so peacefully deep;
And thence unto Liberty, thence unto Gratitude,
   With the third in thy Trinity – Boundless Beatitude:
    Beautiful Spirit of Sleep

Part III

    She ceased: and a deep tingling silence fell
Instantly round, – silence complete, and yet
Instinct as with a breathing sweetness, left
By the rare spirit of her voice foregone:
Even as the Fragrance of a flower were felt
Pervading the mute air, through which erewhile
It had been borne by the delighted hand
Of some sweet-thoughted Maiden. Turning then
Her bright face tow'rds me, as I stood entranced.
Yet with keen wonder stung, she said, 'I love thee!
As first love loveth – utterly! But ah!
This Love itself – this purple-wingèd Love –
This spirit-enriching Spirit of delight,
Is but a honey-bee of Paradise,
That only in the morning glory dares
To range abroad – and when a vagrant most
Adventure out into the common world
Of man and woman; – thither lured by sight
Of some sweet human soul that blooms apart,
Untainted by a rank soil's weedy growths: –
Lured thither thus – yet being, even then,
But wilfully wandering away – away
From its pure birth place (innocent only there!)
And whereunto it must again return,
Or forfeit else its natal passport, – *ere*
The dread night cometh. Yet of how great worth
Is all foregone affection? In the spring
Of even the lowliest love, how many rich
And gracious things that could not else have been,
Grow up like flowers, and breathe a perfume forth
That never leaves again the quickened sense
It once hath hit, as with a fairy's wand,
However fanciful may seem at last
The charm through which it came.' And having said
These mystic sentences, so wild and sweet,
And memorably mournful, – lo, her eyes
Ran o'er with lustres as they opened up
Under mine own now melancholy gaze.

And thus we stood, turned one unto the other,
Till Love again grew glad even from the rich
And wine-like luxury and voluptuous worth
Of its own tear-showers, shed as from the heart!
Forth then once more we looked – silently happy:
Alas! not long: for with a short low gasp
Of sudden fear, she started; nor might I
Stand unalarmed. For hark! within the Tower,
A sound of strenuous steps approaching fast,
Rang upward, as it seemed, from the hard slabs
Of a steep-winding stair; and soon the huge
And brazen portal that behind us shut,
Burst open! with a clang of loosened bolts –
A clang like thunder, that went rattling out
Against the echoes of the distant hills.

With deafened ears and looks aghast, I turned
Tow'rds the harsh noise – there to behold, between
The mighty jambs in the Tower-wall from which
The door swung inward, a tremendous Form!
A horrid gloomy form! That shapeless seemed,
And yet, in its so monstrous bulk, to Man
A hideous likeness bare! Still more and more
Deform it grew, as forth it swelled, and then
Its outlines, shadowing forward, so were lost
On all sides in a grizzly haze, that hung
Vaguely about them, – even as dull grey clouds
Beskirt a coming Tempest's denser mass,
That thickens still internally, and shows
The murkiest in the midst – yea, murkiest there
Where big with fate, and hid in solid gloom,
The yet-still spirit of the thunder broods,
And menaces the world. So dread that Form!

Meanwhile, beholding it, the Lady of light
Had rushed to my extended arms, and hid
Her beamy face, fright-harrowed, in my bosom!
And thus we stood, made one in fear; while still
That terrible Vision out upon us glared
With horny eyeballs – horrible the more
For that no evidence of conscious will,
Or touch of passion, vitalised their fixed
Eumenidèan, stone-cold stare, as tow'rds
Some surely destined task they seemed to guide
Its shapeless bulk and pitiless strength along.

Then with a motion as of one dark stride
Shadowing forward, and outstretching straight
One vague-seen arm, from my reluctant grasp
It tore the radiant Lady, muttering 'This
Is love forbidden!' in a voice whose tones
Were like low guttural thunders heard afar,
Outgrowling from the clouded gorges wild
Of neighboring mountains, when a sultry storm
Is pondering in its dark pavilions there,
And concentrating, like a hill-born host,
Ere it rush valeward; and, as suddenly,
Seized by the other, I was backward thrown
Within the Tower, and heard ere I could rise
From the cold platform, the huge brazen door
Drawn harshly grating to; its beamlike bar
Dropt, with a wall-quake, and the bolts all shot
Into their sockets with a shattering jar!

   I may not paint the horrible despair
That froze me now: (more horrible than aught
In actual destiny, whether bonds or death,
Could give the self-possession of my soul,
If wide awake.) I listened. All was still!
Within – without; – all silent, stirless, cold!
What was my doom? And where was she, my late
So luminous delight? Gone! Reft away
So strangely, terribly! and I myself,
For some all-unimaginable cause,
A dungeoned wretch! Time, every drip of which
Was as an age, kept trickling on, but there
Brought no release – no hope; – brought not a breath
That spake of fellowship, or even of life,
Out of myself – my lonely self! I stood
Utterly blank – utterly shrunken up,
In marble-cold astonishment of heart!
And when at length I cast a desperate look –
A look so desperate that the common gift
Of vision stung me like a deadly curse –
Up and around, pure pity of myself
So warmed and loosened from my brain the pent
And icy anguish, that its load at once
Came, like an alp-thaw, streaming through mine eyes;
Till resignation, that so balmy sweet
Meek flower of Grief which hath its root in tears,

Grew out of mine, – and leisure therewithal
To inspect my prison, whether weak or strong.

   It was a lofty Cell, half round, and had,
Massively set within the crossing wall
That seemed to cut the Tower's whole round in twain,
A second door – shut, and all clamped with brass,
And rough with rows of monstrous iron studs,
And which might haply have thence opened in
Athwart some stairway (as I guessed) that led
Down through the Tower; and by the side of this
A bat-wing'd Steed on scaly dragon claws —
A strange, mute, mystic, almost terrible Thing,
Stood rigid, with a tripod near it placed.
Bare were the dull and ragged walls, but pierced
High out of reach by two small ports that looked
Eastward and westward. As I noted these,
Full on my sight a transient sunbeam fell
Slantingly through, and glowed on the damp floor
A moment, like a streak of burning blood,
Then vanished: wherefore in my heart I guessed
That o'er the mountain tops the sun was then
Oceanward sinking mid the fiery clouds.

   By sure and palpable degrees the night
Came on, and the Cell darkened. Yea, I saw
The Steed and tripod – all its furniture –
Fade, melting gradually, more and more,
Into the darkness, even as a fish,
Through the dense medium of its element,
Retiring down, is in its outlines seen
More shadowy – till 'tis lost. Then all was black.
And to and fro I paced, hour after hour,
And heard my step, the only sound to me
In all the wide world, throb with a dull blow
Down through the hollow Tower that seemed to yawn
Immeasurably beneath, – as it were
A monstrous well whose wide waste mouth was bridged
By that dull-quaking strip of floor alone
On which I darkling strode. Yet on I kept
Pacing, though horrified. Hour after hour
Passed as if clotting at the heart of Time –
Each an eternity of wild expectation,
And weary astonishment! – hour after hour!

And yet no other sound had being there,
Though, as I knew, one live, unmoving Thing
So near me stood in that blind solitude –
Stood waiting – wherefore? by the inner door.

Part IV

   At last, all suddenly, in the air aloft,
O'er the Tower-roof, a wild, weird, wailful song
Woke flying, many-voiced; – then sweeping off
Out tow'rds the echoey hills, so passed away
In dying murmurs through the hollow dark.

Song

    In vain were our spells wrought –
    In vain was She well taught
How that dread Watcher's eyes drowsy to keep;
    In vain was the Dragon-steed
    There at the hour of need,
Out with his double-freight blissward to sweep.

    Lost – lost – lost – lost!
In vain were our spells all of infinite cost!
    Lost – lost – lost – lost –
Yon Gulf by a mortal may be crossed *never!*
    Never – ah never!
    The doom holds for ever!
    For ever! for ever!

    Lost – lost – lost – lost!
    Come away – come away.
Since only in soul yon vague Gulf can be crost,
Our beautiful Mistress her failure must weep –
    Weep – weep – weep – weep!
    Away – come away!
For see, wide uprolling, the white front of day!
Away to the mystic mid-regions of Sleep –
    Of the beautiful Spirit of Sleep!

    Lost – lost – lost – lost –
The Gulf *we* are crossing, may never be crost
    By a Mortal – ah, never!
    The dooms holds for ever!
      For ever! for ever!

So passed that Song: (of which the drift alone
Is here reached after in such leaden speech
As uncharmed mortals use.) And when its tones
Out tow'rds the mountains in the dark afar,
Had wasted, I grew sensible, methought,
Of seasonable change; – that now the Cell
Kept clarifying till the darkness seemed
Marbled with grey; and then the Steed again,
With his strange dragon-claws and half-spread wings,
And eke the tripod, where it still had stood,
Figured like shadows through the thinning gloom,
And gradually thence, by just the same
Degrees reversed in which they'd faded there
Into the darkness as the night advanced,
Came forth in full development again.

It was the Dawn: and thus it clearing kept,
Till through the eastern port a golden rod
Of light fell transiently, and so bespake
The sunrise! Oh, it was a desolate pass,
To feel, – immured in that relentless Keep, –
How on the purple hills the sun was then
Rejoicing in his glory! Then to know
That he was wheeling up the heaven, and o'er
My prison-roof; – hour after hour, to think
How he was tracking with a step of fire
His midway course, and loudening through the world
The thunder of its universal life!
Or how his mighty orb had sloped in Time's
Descending scale, and thence was glorying down
Into the crimson waves of some wide sea
Beyond the Hesperides! But this, alas!
Was my dread fate while seven times day and night
So wearily came, – so wore away; and yet
I slept not! nor (to my amazement) there,
Through all this drear time, did the wintry tooth
Of hunger gnaw within my corporal frame!
No thirst inflamed me! While by the grim door
Which seemed to shut athwart some stairway, stood
That strange, unmoving, dragon-footed Steed,
As from the first, – and there the tripod, placed
As if to aid some fugitive to mount
At once – and fly! Mere wonder at my doom,
So unimaginably wild and vague,

Relieved the else-fixed darkness of despair.

  But on the seventh night, in the stillness, – hark!
What might I hear? A step? – a small light step,
That by the stair ascending, swiftly came
Straight to the inner door – then stopt. Alas!
The black leaf opened not; and yet, the while,
In evidence of some bright Being that out
Beyond it stood, a rainbow radiance through
Its solid breadth, in subtle wave on wave,
Came flushing, – even as a sunset glow
Through some dense cloud upon the verge of heaven,
In swift rich curves wells percolating forth;
So came it – filling all the Cell at length
With rosy lights that in the darkness fumed
Like luminous odors; at the scent of which,
The mystic Steed, so rigid until then,
Moved, and spread wide his glimmering bat-like wings.
When hark! deep down in the mysterious Tower,
Another step? Yea, the same strenuous tramp
That once before I'd heard big-beating up,
Came following – till a low sad cry without
Went to my heart, and I might hear ensue
A struggle as of one forced down the stair
By that so ruthless Guard! – down, till the Cell
Again had darkened, and the Tower itself
Stood once more as in some mute void of Time,
Or depth of distance infinitely out,
Achingly still. But not for long! Again
The Monster's hateful tramp came booming up,
Quake above quake that with a shudder stopt
Dead at the door. It opened; and he stood
In dubious presence 'twixt the mighty jambs,
Filling the whole wide space. But ere the Fiend
Might enter farther, rage and hate at once
Possessed me, and I charged him! For awhile
His horrible glooms voluminously vague,
Yet with a smothering pressure in their folds,
Involved me! – concentrating more and more,
And lapping closer in yet denser coils,
Every dread moment! But my agony now,
My pain, and hate, and loathing, – all had grown
Into so vast a horror, that methought
I burst with irresistible strength away!

Rushed through the door, and down the stairway – down
An endless depth; till a portcullis, hinged
In the Tower's basement, opened to my flight!
No sooner had I passed it, than it fell
In thunder to! and thence my passage lay
Along the difficult ledges of a rock
Against whose base the Lake's long ripple lapped.

  And when at last, breathless and faint, I paused
In that so giddy flight, methought I saw
The lustrous Lady up through the lit air
Ascending, with a steadfast downward look
Of parting recognition, – full of love,
But painless, passionless. Upward she passed,
Above the Tower, and o'er the clouds, – and when
Her radiance melted through heaven's marble dome
And left it vacant in its infinite vastness,
All things methought had changed, and I was there
Standing alone in a wide waste that stretched
On all hands out – illimitably out!
Standing alone in a waste universe,
That showed, as under an abortive dawn,
Its grey immensity, and nothing more!
Still, empty, objectless! – and thereupon
There fell back on my soul a sense of loss
So bleak, so desolate that with a wild
Sleep startling outcry, suddenly I awoke!
Awoke, to find it but a Dream of Wonder!
Yet ever since to feel as if some pure
And guardian Soul, out of the day and night,
Had passed for ever from the reach of Love!
Albeit I know, that to the Poet's mind,
No light, no loveliness it once hath known,
Though only through the mystery of a dream,
Is after lost; but in effect remains,
As comfort, or as wisdom, or as grace,
In union with its substance evermore –
A gathered portion of the life and might
Of *His* predestined influence on the world.

3 • On Social and Spiritual Issues •

Words *Are* Deeds
(from The Nevers of Poetry)

Words *are* deeds. The words we hear
May revolutionise or rear
A mighty state. The words we read
May orb a spiritual deed,
Excelling any fleshly one,
As much as the celestial sun
Transcends a bonfire, made to throw
A light on some mere Raree-show.
A simple proverb, tagged with rhyme,
May colour half the course of time;
The pregnant saying of a sage,
May influence every coming age;
A song in its effects may be
More glorious than Thermopylae:
While a great Book is in my view
A greater *deed* than Waterloo,
And many a lay that schoolboys scan
A nobler feat than Inkerman.

Asinine Loyalty and Abject Patriotism

    To Principles let us be loyal alway,
        And true to all good in Man's general story;
    Not to that bauble called Royal Display,
        And that man eating monster called National Glory.

• ON SOCIAL AND SPIRITUAL ISSUES •

NOTE English loyalty is a moral puzzle, and so is modern English patriotism. To attempt to account for them on rational grounds, or to refer them to any sufficient reason, would be about as vain as to endeavour by a logical process to convert the shape of a mist-heap into that of a steam carriage: so slavish is the one and so unwarranted the other. The best satirical embodiment of both that I have ever met with, is the caricature of a poor fellow who is about to drink at a public fountain from a vessel chained to it for safety. He is depicted as a squalid, shrivelled creature, out at elbows, out at knees, out at breech, out at hat; and, in short, out at all points: and the hungry sharpness of his visage gives a strange, haggard fervency to its expression, while he is supposed to be delivering himself, preparatory to drinking, of the following loyal and patriotic toast:– 'Here's the Queen, God bless her! and old England forever!' Now this much of the matter – the mere surface of it – is only calculated to provoke a smile. But when we look somewhat deeper, the smile becomes sickly, and fades away from us. For there, deep down, as it were, we see that the abject popular tendencies to deify and worship the mere shows of greatness, and to merge all the individual claims of manhood in that of a vast tax-grinding national pretense, and those of a Juggernautic majesty, lie at the very root (if they be not the root itself) of the poor tatterdemalion's misery.

True and False Glory
(from War)

How long shall splendid guilt mankind deceive?
   See furious Conqueror after Conqueror sweep
Over the Past! ambitious each to achieve
   Time's most unrighteous victory, and thence reap
   Unequalled sway, and make their age one heap
Of bloody marvels for slave-bards to weave
Into loud verse; and finally, so leave
   To Glory names that she should blush to Keep!
How greater *they* who tyrants did [repel]
   And yet all public dignities disown
But such as were the means to *serving* well!
   Compare an Alexander's wild renown
   With the fraternal memories that crown
The glory of Hampden, Washington, and Tell.

Wellington

Great captain if you will! great Duke! great Slave!
Great minion of the crown! - but a great man
He *was* not! He? the iron instrument
Of mere authority! the atheist
Of a conventional and most earthy duty!
To whom the powers that be were simply not
Of God - but in His stead! Shall we belie
All righteous instinct and profane all truth,
By calling *great* a man without a soul?
One who, apart from the despotic wills
Of crowned oppressors, knew no right, no wrong,
No faith, no country, and no brotherhood?
If such a man were *great*, may God most High
Spare henceforth to our universal race
All *greatness*, seeing it may sometimes be
A rigid, kindless battlement of Power
Self-throned and sanctioned only by the sword.
And if, as Englishmen are proud to boast,
He was their greatest countryman - alas!
For England's national sterility!
But they who thus belaud him, *lie*, as all
True patriots most feelingly perceive.
Besides, he was not England's son at all:
He was an Irishman, with whom the name
Of Ireland was a scoff! an Irishman,
Who for a hireling's meed and ministry,
Could tear away from his inhuman heart
The pleading image of his native Land.

Edmund Burke

It is, or was till very lately, the literary fashion of England, to style Burke the most philosophic of British statesmen. But methinks such eulogy is hardly wise. At all events, it is not entirely complimentary to the intellectual enlightenment and acumen of the nation. He was scarcely a safe philosopher who could talk as Burke did about French *principles*; and for which he richly merited the sarcasm of Paine, who asked him why he did not also denounce French angles and rhomboids and parallelograms. The sarcasm was cogent: for principles, in the final sense of the term - that sense in which a philosophical statesman should alone use it - can be of no place or time, but of the world, and for ever. To hold that the fact is otherwise, is to confound *notions* with principles. Now a mere notion may be right or wrong, but a veritable principle must be right, always and inevitably, because everlastingly referable to some standard in nature. Neither are *rules* to be confounded with principles; for though apparently wise and expedient, they may be contrary to the ultimate reason of things, and thence more or less pernicious, and to be superseded by the truth. In short, principles are determinate tendencies in the right constitution of things, and we cannot therefore, in any sense, *devise* them. We may devise plans, but we can only hit upon principles; and the proper question to be considered in any mooted matter of right, is not whether it be of French or English, or even of Russian origin, but whether it be truly a principle. Thus, it is an indubitable principle in the constitution of humanity, that all men are (that is, should be) born equally free, as being all equally the children of God, and all equally sanctioned by the mould of Nature; and whatever, therefore, is repugnant to this, in the political constitution of any state or people, must be purely a *device*, and manifestly a wrong. But Burke would not see the matter in this light; or perhaps he could not so see it through the dazzling medium of a pension in prospect. He was a better orator than philosopher. But even his oratory appears to me to be always overstrained, often bombastic, and degraded by its verbiage to a secondary result. It exhibits a total want of what may be called epical simplicity. Gravity it has, but it is the gravity of a bedizened pagod. Hence I cannot altogether relish even his best and most admired passages – nay, not even his most startling and far-famed *bursts*. They are too like theatrical tempests, all noise and wildfire, and robustious effort: wanting in analogies to the awful pauses and unobvious preparations, the terribly sudden explosions, and all the greatly simple grandeurs that most affect us in the elemental commotions of Nature: so that he who has ever witnessed an actual storm amid echoing mountains or in the depths of a hoarsely-resounding forest, cannot be heartily moved by such tempestuous mockeries – except, perhaps, to laughter. And moreover, these best things of Burke, with all their splendor, are too often the sophistic gilding of an untruth, or of but the time-serving half of a very truth, the other half being suppressed for the occasion. I would strongly advise youngsters not to take for gospel all that British critics are wont to say about the merits of Edmund Burke. It is the conservative loyalty and the aristocratical tenor of his writings, with their specious claptrap about chivalry and the 'cheap defence of nations,' that give such unction and grandiloquence to the eulogiums of these critics. Yet Burke himself could be democratic enough, (at least in spirit) and look far into the mystery of an ancient iniquity when his own personal corns happened to be trodden upon, though by a Duke of Bedford. But the truth is, he had set his heart upon a plentiful pension, and knew the road to it.

I doubt not the boldness of such criticism as the above, will be objected to *in me*. It will be denounced no doubt by many, as a sort of rebellious manifesto, dashed recklessly against the authority of the British Stagirites, past and present. So be it. In such a matter, I can acknowledge but one great authority – the Truth, or what I believe to be the Truth. – Hence (so to speak) I have no literary solicitude. Disposed in the first place to regard only the truth, I can naturally dispose myself in the second to wish even my own verdicts to become current only in the event of their being either elucidatory or suggestive of it – and of it alone. Within this pale I have no fear, and without it, I ask no favor.

On the Repeal Movement in Ireland

Since every drop of wrong-shed blood that cries
Out of the lapse of ages, at the throne
Of God is heard, still present; since the lies
Of fraudulent Power are mortal, and the groan
Of patriot Grief smites not as against stone
At Nature's heart, though hardened; since the sighs
Of beggared love, roofed only by the skies,
Must weary Mercy with perpetual moan;
Since Right *is* on the earth, and doth belong
To heaven as well, crushed Ireland yet shall cast
Far off the burthen she has borne so long;
Calling retributive thunder from the Past
To speak her will, and swell the trumpet-blast
Of Liberty triumphant over Wrong.*

* He but profanes the spirit of patriotism in his pretensions thereto, whose fraternal sympathies are not co-extensive with humanity, and wide as the world, however they may primarily centre amongst his own countrymen, and in the land of his nativity. Nay, wherever Truth obtains with the greatest certainty, and rectitude of conduct prospers most universally, – thither still should our sympathies tend as to our better country – the Country of Man: or to fold the principle in another soul-born faculty, there is often much pain, arising from the consciousness of our having become worse; – less generous, less devotional, less loving (in an unselfish sense). Alas! in the great majority of cases, to have become elderly is to have made entire shipwreck of the Spiritual. To have lived fifty years is almost inevitably to have arrived at that sad pass in which the Material is alone sought after and believed in. Strange! that the more we have experience of the precarious and unsatisfactory nature of all merely earthly things, that we should yet grow to them more and more: that the further we

travel heavenward, our spirits, once so erect like our bodies, should contract like these more and more of a tendency to stoop dustward. But such is the case, and whence is it? Mainly from the influence of a corrupt civilisation, the wisdom of which is only and continually of the earth earthy; and which (so insidious is it) the generosity of youth can alone counteract for the time – and for thus long in but a very few individuals. The great lump of nascent humanity is destitute even of this leven – it is bred out of it. But there is a better time coming.

Whatever Is, Is Right
(No. 9 in A String of Passing Thoughts)

When Pope declared, Whatever Is, is Right,
Had he been whipped until he bled,
Then salved with his own words in merry spite,
I wonder what he *could* have said?

NOTE The above doctrine of Pope is about as exquisite an absurdity as ever was written. It is even worse than absurd, being an arrant piece of moral quietism. It is even worse again than moral quietism, being a justification as well as a toleration of any and every kind of existing abuse. Were it indeed the great obvious Truth that he proclaims it to be, it were no matter whatsoever he might might do; because, when done, it would be only a part of *whatever is*, and *consequently* right. True, there would be the same argument for whatever might be done counteractively. But this were only to confess and prolong the absurdity.

A similar fallacy lies couched in the saying, 'The Powers that Be are of God.' Of course he permits them or they could not be. He may sanction them, but he does not directly institute them. They are, in their origin, the probational structures of men, though obtaining both in their beginning and continuance, by the Divine sanction or sufferance: and they may, therefore, be either morally right or morally wrong, or partake more or less of both conditions. If right, God favors them; if wrong, he suffers them: because the highest public heroism can only be mightily evinced by their counter existence. The powers that be are of God, then, only in so far as they co-exist with his moral government of the world; – permissively, if bad, for the oppositional exercise of public virtue; and by favor or adoption, if good, as the highest result of it. Hence, as it is noble to obey all just laws, and to support all righteous rule, so is it not only optional, but meritorious, to resist and subvert, if possible, all flagrant and mischievous authority.

A Bit of Prose in the Vein and After the Manner of the Hon. Robert Boyle

Lice are appointed unto beggars, whereby they may be subject to an appropriate chastisement, under the providential law which ordaneth that all men shall be born unto trouble, even as the sparks do fly upwards. The said lice are thus peculiarly appointed unto beggars, because only for the plague of them, so long as they could circumvent a little food, and a rag to wear (which they mostly can), they would (like even to brute beasts) be perfectly careless and contented (speaking of them in the main) seeing that if ever they had or would have cared for aught besides or beyond they would surer [not] have come to a pass so vile as that of beggary, living as they do in a vast workshop (the Earth) wherein all who will are able to sustain themselves by the labor of their own hands or the application of their own minds. And herein may we perceive the marvellous wisdom of Providence, which ever chasteneth us in the manner best calculated to reach us through those very dispositions and habits which do chiefly constitute the temper and mode of our moral nature and social existence.

Satire

The vulgar Satirist I detest! The mean
Detractor is, of all vile things that crawl
Loathsome and poisonous 'twixt earth and heaven,
What least, from impulse and the bent of thought,
I would be neighbour to. But when the Rights
Of Man are trampled on: when Villains sit,
In the high places of the Land, and scoff
At all the just hold sacred: when mere pelf,
No matter how acquired, alone can win
The plaudits of its Nestors, and the sleek
Respect even of the *pious*: – then the scorn
Of Indignation, with its brave disgust,
Put forth in tones that burst like Jove's own thunder,
Are good, are godly – Scoundrels never feel them.*

---

* A sickly tendency to repudiate the power and office of Satire has been somewhat laboriously manifested by several modern poets of prime note otherwise. Now this seems to me to have indicated in them a defective moral consciousness rather than a transcendent one, notwithstanding much fine-woven theory to the contrary, from the pens both of themselves and their admirers – unless indeed, it could be proven at

the same time, that there were no longer any wrongs in the world but such as can be castigated by Law; nor any men like those of whom Pope spoke, when he said he felt his satirical ministry of some service, seeing that *many who are not afraid of God were afraid of him*. There is a *convenient* complacency which is anything but genuine. And they who are loving-king and long-suffering 'in the lump', have usually but little of either to spare for particular cases that may happen, where true charity begins, – at or near home. There is also a commercial sort of purist who is anything but a fit model for a hearty-spirited poet to square his social humanities by. Most mercifully disposed towards great sinners and great sins, he is ever ready to hunt down small ones with a full cry of moral indignation. To give a 'modern instance' of his peculiar genius he considers a pecuniary defaulter to the vulgar tune of some hundred pence, a rascal upon whom lenity would be thrown away; while another who backslides from under the responsibility of as many thousand pounds, is at the worst, he thinks, – only an *unfortunate gentleman*. And while society is overstocked even with cattle of this kedney, – to probe its constitution no further, – shall we be told that there is no *call* for Poetical Satire. 'Throw *such* physic to the dogs – I'll none of 't!'

Marvellous Martin

I

An old draught of him (from an unpublished satire)
    As a new-fledged attorney and sub-editor.

    I looked, and saw a low-browed Creature pass,
A sort of mule, 'twixt human fox and ass;
Half to his face he held a mask, and so
Read from a broad-sheet, sneeringly and slow:
For genuine malice in a nature cold
Is sly and slinking, never quick and bold,
    You know him, Truth resumed; but none but he
Himself can know how mean a *man* may be,
And yet retain Man's likeness! Let him sneer;
'Tis the vile solace of a vile career.

Just loosed from school, and learned enough to string
Rote-beads from Horace, he dished up a thing
Y-clept a Book by custom, as the one
Wide term of dog takes in each bitch's son:
Full of mere words; without one glow of joy,
One gush of love, though written by a *boy!*
'Tis dead long since: – And now, by Faction hired,
That is, by just two pounds per week inspired,
Lo, guarded by the mask that erst was Lowe's,
He churns and spits his venom as he goes
On what the brave admire, the truthful laud,
As raised by merit and unstained with fraud,
And thence on all whom his base spirit knows
Must be, by destiny, his *human* foes!

II

    A new draught of him,
      As a self-nominated senator, and sub-constitutionalist

Who sees him walk the street, can scarce forebear
To question thus his friend. What prig goes there?
So much hath Nature, as 'tis oft her plan,
Stamped inward trickery on the outward man!
And yet, with her great interdiction deep
Impressed thus on his being, see him creep
Into our Parliament, and dare to prate
About the god-like principles of State;
With this sole claim address him to the work,
That he has read that prince of sophists, Burke!
And though a dreary Plunkett's glad to praise
His talents, seeing that their feeble rays
Have just that kindred with his own pinched mind
Which (says the proverb) makes us wond'rous kind.
No more could such a creature feel or think
Beyond Expediency's most beaten brink,
Or sum the onward pressure of our race,
Than I could heave a mountain from its base!
Nay, even the dogmas of his vaunted Burke
Work in him to no end, or backward work,
Or dwindle in his view, like heaven's wide cope
Seen through the wrong end of a telescope.

How then might such a 'thing', with all the gang
That yet like vermin about Wentworth hang,
Rear-ranked with hirelings, – how might he and these,
(Any-thing snobs* and no-thing Nominees!)
Devise a Government intoned and twined
With all that's true and fetterless in mind
And free in body – one, in short, designed
Not for the pigmies of the passing hour,
But for Australia's future sons of Power?
No! they can spin but feudal cobwebs, soon
By Freedom to be blown into the moon,
Or back to Norfolk Island, whence, 'tis plain,
Their slimy embryos came in youthful Lottery's brain.

*Or rather, fellows who, in a lordly direction, would be anything but what they are – conscious snobs. I, for one, will henceforth wage quarterless war with the whole gang; at least in *words* till a true occasion offer, and then by *deeds* also. I have been slow to draw against them my satirical sword, but I have studied the entire debate on the New Constitution, and *now*, having drawn it, I throw away the scabbard.

This war of public opinion with party interest will not be a very long one. The designers and their designs are at length unmasked, and this is just what was most wanted – the 'one thing needful' to the liberal cause. And if I am not strangely mistaken, the star of the whole gang's political destiny is fast setting – and for ever. The Bunyip *was*, and *is*, and is *to be* – nothing. So of them.

However, should the rascally Consititution in question be ultimately sanctioned by the British Government, – then every liberal in the colony, who has not something slavish at the bottom of his nature, will have nothing for it but to keep his powder dry, and a sharp look out for the best vantage ground . . .

As to the qualification of members for either house – their election by the people should be the sole test of their eligibility. At all events there should be no property qualification. And in the great Australian Consitution yet to be fashioned in the good time coming, by the born sons of the soil, there shall be no requirement so barbarous. What has the property to do with the brain-power of legislation? Can it think? Can it even labour of itself to a national end? It can do neither. Strip it of man, and it is morally nothing. Attach it to human dishonesty or non-intelligence, and it is morally vicious. But then it is urged that it gives to its possessors the feeling of having a permanent stake in the country. Now, to a certain extent, it must be admitted that it does: and yet all history proves that the only vitally efficient bond between a people and their country, is that pure love of it which is natural to the unvitiated human heart, and which, of mere consequence, must be best cherished by a citizenship devoid of all arbitrary inequalities and invidious distinctions. Besides, who have so great a stake in their country as they who are too poor to shift out of it – too moneyless to buy a secure asylum in another? To whom, in short, through the mere lack of transferable riches, their own country and the well-being of it is all in all.

Yet property, wealth, whatever exempts from labour on the one hand, and commands it on the other, will always have its due weight as a social influence, in virtue of its relation to the well-being of man. And let it always have this weight (for it *will* have it), but not a grain more.

from The Temple of Infamy

(In a vision the poet is conducted by a beautiful woman to observe a pageant of the wrong and infamy enacted in his native land. The progress of error climaxes with the appearance of the squatters and their leader, William Charles Wentworth. (Ed.))

But hark! what hubbub now is this that comes
Straight for the portal? Oaths and threats like lomes [lambs, OED].
Exploding, till that in full force and feather
March the Squatocracy, with their bell-wether!
Even thus, insane of hope, the Prince of Evil
Marshalled his luckless followers – to the Devil!

   First come the Magnates – mark their Leader, he,
The would be Tell of the Fraternity!
His state is that, so infamously sad,
Where Talent hath through selfishness run mad.
In his well-masked display of by-gone years,
With democratic wrath he tore the ears
Of Sydney's wealthiest groundlings, being then
Thwarted and snubbed by Darling's party-men!
But now behold him in his native hue,
The bullying, bellowing, champion of the Few!
A Patriot? – he who hath nor sense nor heed!
Of public ends beyond his *own* mere need!
Whose Country's ruin, to his public fear,
Means only this – the loss of Windermere!
And by the same self legislature rule,
Australia's growth the growth of W-tw-th's wool!
Her rights – her liberties, for number *one*
A Patriot? – *he* from whose statistic care
All that his Country's general homes should bear
Of mind and happiness, is thrust by that
Which by some process may be turned to fat,
And, duly barrelled and exported, then
Return in *wine* for grazier *gentlemen!*

Such is yon Man! and not a whit belied!
A Patriot? Let him 'doff that lion's hide'!
Well may those Landsharks call him their pure Gem
For bound thus to *himself*, he's bound to *them*.

A Roguish Epigram

The most accomplished Rogue is one
Who best can mask the roguery done;
Not he who plans with greatest skill
The means whereby to compass ill.

from Sonnets Dedicated to Australian Senators

I
Is Wentworth a Patriot?

Licence they mean when they cry Liberty.
Who loves that must first be wise and good.

Milton

A Patriot is one who hath no aims
   Dividual from the Public Good; whose heart
   Is of his Country's a fraternal part;
Whose Interest on that Country's altar flames.
A Patriot is one who hath no Self
   Dividual from his People – tell me then,
   Is Wentworth such amongst Australia's Men?
Where Hampden's wisdom? Marvell's scorn of pelf?
What though a Faction's magnates when they're mellow
   Trumpet him forth a Patriot? What though all
The 'Brandy-faced', when they behold him, bellow
   'A Patriot'? Yet, however loud he bawl
   About his Country, 'twere as fit to call
Maize dumpling gold, because forsooth – 'tis yellow.

IX
'It's No Go!'

> Buy a broom – buy a broom!
> Who'll buy a broom?
>
> *Popular Song*

How stript of all that giveth Life to glow
  Becomes the light of Day's illustrious lamp,
  Ere it can pierce into the chambers damp
Of yon old law-be-lumbered Pile!* and so,
Poor Foster, shorn of all its warmth and dim,
  Must Truth become ere it can passage find
  Amid the legal cobwebs of thy mind,
Grown old in word-craft, and propense to trim!
Hence all thy vacillation – all thy twaddle –
  Thy would-and-would-not – speaking now – now dumb!
Give up at once, man! For a head so addle
What Government on Earth would give a crumb,
Much less a Place? and in the *Patriot's* ladle,
  Thou seest, there's nothing touchable for scum!

* The old Court House, King Street.

from Bits

No. LXXXI
On hearing that Sir Charles Nicholson was Going to England

So Sir Charles goeth home, with his coals to Newcastle,
  That is, with his Title, since with him it goes;
And there it may suit, as a personal tassel,
  Though *here* it appeared just as silly to those
  Who dare think, as the reed in a Blackfellow's nose,
Whereby he would hint the sublime estimation,
In which he is held (by *himself*) in his nation.

No. XVII
Capital Punishment

To string a man up for the very worst crime,
Is like smashing a watch for not keeping good time:
   It were wiser no doubt,
To use the bad man in a work of some good
   And so patent a moral sublime;
   And, by cleaning it out,
To make the wrong watch keep the best time we could: –
   What is this but the truth – *though in rhyme?*

No. XI
To a Girl Who Stole a Young Apple Tree

Alas! from the beginning,
In the records of all sinning
No comparative may grapple
   With a culprit like to thee!
Eve herself but stole an apple –
   You have filched an Apple Tree!

The Big (Bygone) Claims of the Big Squatters

No small share of the credit of arming public opinion against the monstrous claims that were entertained by the great Squatters some nine or ten years since, is due even to *me*. Their claims, I say, as they were first divulged at a memorable meeting in the Royal Hotel, were then perfectly monstrous, comprehending nothing less than the *fee simples* of their immense Runs. Indeed, 'To us and to our heirs for ever' became thenceforth for some time, a sort of camp *shibboleth* with a large and powerful section of the squatocracy. Well, *if not the first*, I was certainly amongst the first, to apprehend the devilish evils that were clouding up in the probable future from these monstrous claims: and at once waged a merciless war against them, both in prose and rhyme, – till they toned down wonderfully. And this I did, without one ray of encouragement, or one rag of personal benefit, from any quarter whatever. Still I did not slacken a whit in my opposition to them, both in public and private, by articles in newspapers and letters to individuals, till I thought I could assure myself of their ultimate frustration. But to the immediate purpose of this note: perhaps the most popularly telling things which I then threw forth against them, were a series of 'Squatter Songs,' that appeared from time to time in the *Weekly Register*, a liberal journal long since defunct. The following is one of these effusions, written in ridicule of the overweening dislike which the greater would-be aristocratic squatters were very forward in evincing towards their smaller and more plebeanish *brethren*: and though somewhat aside from the main matter, I republish it as a specimen. In doing so, I shall be re-fighting as it were, a battle of the past; but the pith of the thing, will, I think, justify the indulgence.

Tom Brown, or Haman in the Bush*

I had a noble Station once as any in the land
Its hills were free from *gibbas*, its valleys void of sand;
But what of this? since if I rode three miles the creek adown.
There sat, like Mordecai the Jew – one curst Tom Brown!

>   Tom Brown, who
>   With his five mile of a run.
>   Cut my hundred thousand acre one
>   Almost in two.

I courted the Commissioner, I feasted him; and when
He praised my finest pony, I gave it to him then:
I gave it to him, hoping he would aid me in the *down*
I had upon the Station of – this curst Tom Brown!

>   Tom Brown, who, &c.

But ah! that false Commissioner, he failed me at the last!
Tom Brown remained and flourished, while I was breaking fast!
My Station grew so hateful then, I came to live in town,
And took to grog, and dice, and all – through that Tom Brown!

>   Tom Brown, who, &c.

At last I sold my Right of Run; – and now with nought to do,
And still a little money – I drink till all is blue!
And lo, the grimmest of the Fiends that haunt me up and down,
Is like – ev'n in its blueness like! – that d-d Tom Brown;

>   Tom Brown, who
>   With his five mile of a run,
>   Cut my hundred thousand acre one
>   Almost in two.

(* Haman – an overreaching minister who, in seeking to destroy the chosen people, set himself against the will of God and was destroyed. See Book of Esther 3-7. (Ed.))

Bush Justice
from Squatter Songs No. VI

A Dealer, bewitched by gain-promising dreams,
Settled down near my Station, to trade with the Teams,
And to sell to the shepherds! from whom, through the nose,
Until then, I had screw'd just what prices I chose;
And for this, to be sure, I so hated the man,
That I swore ne'er to rest till I'd settled some plan
   Whereby in the Lockup to cleverly cram him!
And so to my Super the matter I put,
Who thereupon 'found' a sheep's head near his hut,
   And the 'how came it there?' was sufficient to damn him,
The Beak before whom I then lugg'd him, as you
May suppose, being neck-deep in Squattery too.

'Twas a beautiful Hearing, as noted at large
By the Clerk (who was bonuss'd) – sheep-stealing the charge;
'Twould make your hearts laugh in the Records to see
How we bullied him out of his wits! – I say *we*,
Because while on this side against him I banged,
On the other the Beak said he ought to be hanged
   For a gallow-grained, scandalous son of transgression!
And committing him then – the case being so plain,
We sent him three hundred miles 'down on the chain'
   To his Trial – and eke his 'acquittal', at Session!
For what care we Squatters for Law on a push?
And for Justice! what has she to do with the Bush?

A Splendid is Never a Happy Land

No: a splendid is never a happy Land! While it flames, as it were a reversed sky, with starred nobles and jewelled ladies, it swarms yet more abundantly, as a rotting carcase does with the lower forms of life, – with criminals and outcasts. And this great heaven-mocking disparity of social condition grew, at first, out of an unjust division of the lands, however remotely as an effect it may subsequently refer to this its primal cause. Immense equalities in the proprietorships of its soil are the arch curses of England, giving birth to two national monsters, – a heartless magnificence in the rich and a social hopelessness in the poor, which become in turn the parents of an audacious denial of the common claim of humanity in the one class, and a sullen distrust even of God's providence in the other, which 'cannot love (it is thought) the wretch it starves' - yes, starves in the midst of abundance! Such is the state of England. And, where-ever, in any society, there are hereditary Pariahs, something radically fraudulent in the structure of that society is the cause of the evil. Were it or could it be otherwise, the blame would be with Providence. But God is just.

No: a splendid is never a happy land. Wherever there are palaces there are hovels: and this should determine us in Australia to have as few of either as possible; for the first are but the glaring evidences of political imposition, the social cost of which is indicated, and *reproached* by the inevitable neighbourhood of the latter. Nay, wherever *mansions* are very frequent, and gentlemen, in the useless sense of the term, exceedingly plentiful, there also poor-houses abound, the energy of the labourer serves but to keep him from his rest in the grave, every town has its Pariah quarter, and unconfessing paupers starve together in heaps. Such, universally, is the condition of England, and our present and future legislators should perpetually propound to themselves the question, whether the same national enormities - a bloated patrimonial pomp on the one hand, and hereditary destitution on the other - are to be extended to Australia? By keeping this constantly at heart, they will assuredly grow up to the conception of something better.

On the Proposed Recurrence to Transportation from Miscellaneous Sonnets No. XXV

The shame of bondage is upon the Land
Even yet; and a wild cry of blood complains
To Heaven, like Abel's, whereso bushward band
The myrmidons of *their* polluted gains
Who erst drove Mammon's chariot scourge in hand!
And shall they *again*, to puff their windy shows
Of Lordship; spot us with the plague of those
Who would perpetuate the shameful brand -
The accusing cry* - and thence through labor's fee,
Cheapen our Manhood! Better that this fair
New world once more a wilderness should be!
Or that the cause of such unrighteous care,
Our cattle, like the swine of Gadara, were
Devil-entered all and drownèd in the sea!

* In the earlier Colonial times, when the remote Squattages were mostly manned by assigned convicts, the Blacks of those regions were usually treated by them with great licentiousness and oppression. And if they happened to be somewhat resentful under this sort of civilized treatment – but especially if, from whatever cause, they became at all 'troublesome' (as the phrase went) to the *cattle*, by eating a beast occasionally, in lieu of a kangaroo, or by in anywise routing or unsettling a herd when gathered upon some chosen camping-ground, though by their inopportune presence only – then, these convict servants, on the merest hint from their Sydney-dwelling masters, as to the desirableness of their doing so, were wont to slaughter them with as little scruple as if they were accounting, in the same bloody fashion, for so many dingoes. I have myself seen as many as nine convict stockmen hanged in Sydney, in one bunch, for the wholesale massacre of a tribe of Blacks, having been incited thereto, as was generally believed at the time, by their master or masters; though the misguided stockmen, by dying *game*, carried this damning secret away with them. But whither? Such a question can be even glanced at, *only* with a shudder.

Aboriginal Death Song

Behold, it is the camp-fire of our Brother! –
But I see only in the ring of its light
A weeping woman with a young child,
And look in vain for the gleam of the tomahawk
That but yesterday was merry in the tree-tops.

The fish-pools of the ancient river
Have lost the shadow of a skilful hand!
The well-known tracks of a fleet-footed hunter
Are fast fading from the grassy hills,
And a sure spear of the tribe is broken.

There is a vacant place in the circle of the Seers:
From the consultations of the wise and brave
A bold voice has gone up forever!
And a whoop that late was loud on our border
Is terrible only in the deeds of the past.

My Sable Fair

The Maidens of Bushton are rare and bright,
Have forms for sculpture, and souls for delight,
With wiles to witch one, and smiles to please,
And tears that are even more sweet than these:
But turning from all, though thus bright and rare,
I follow my heart to my Sable Fair.

Dark is her cheek, but the rich blood's ray
Glows through its night with the warmth of day;
While Joy, like a bird of passion, sips
The love-ripe dew of her smiling lips,
And her wild eyes shine, like twin-stars rare,
Out from a cloud of glossy hair.

And ever I pride in my Forest choice
The more while I list to her bird-like voice,
Warbling old songs in her own wild speech
With this burden new to each:
'Who will pity the Dark-wing'd Dove,
When her white Hawk leaves her to die of love?'

O then, by the artless tears that rise
'Neath the downcast lids of her gleaming eyes;
By the truthfully tender and touching grace
That boding passion then lends her face;
In the depths of my yearning soul, I swear
Never to leave her – my Sable fair!

NOTE This poem was suggested by the following passage (extracted by permission) in a private letter.

It is indeed true, that young *** has openly attached himself to an aboriginal girl here, though, as you observe, he stood A.1. in the graces of some of the finest belles in — ; a fact certainly, which in nowise tends to his excuse. Yet, I can assure you, the *sable fair one* who has thus bewitched him, is quite a Bush Cleopatra, possessing much striking though wild beauty. To see her in motion, is immediately to bethink one of a black antelope, or of some graceful wild creature of the sort; while her head of hair on the poll of an Opera dancer (to say the very least of it) were predestined to a coronet.

The Poem itself has been censured as being too impassioned for the subject too glossy; and as showing the Poet to have entered too *con amore* also into the color of its circumstances. But such conventional cant is easily 'sent to Coventry'. The Poet's theme was granted love, and what has its wild spirit, when once evoked, to do with the accident of a black or white skin? That subtile power of passion which cometh as unbiddenly as the 'breath of the sweet South over a bed of violets, stealing and giving odours,' and finding 'Helen's beauty in a brow of Egypt' – what careth it, I would ask, in the presence of its object, for arbitary proprieties? And was the Poet, with these questions at his heart, to caution the Muse, notwithstanding, against skipping over the clipt-hedge-like limits of modern literary gentility? I mean that small straight laced sentimental sort of verse-test which obtains so mightily amongst learned old maids and Montgomery-reading bachelors. But the words quoted above from Shakespear, are alone suggestive of an answer sufficiently conclusive – and I consider the objections, therefore, as 'sent to Coventry'.

Charity

Man were a grinding niggard, lean and hoar
Even in his youth, and in his riches poor,
Didst thou ne'er leave thy blessing at his door,
If not from Thee, whence were there balm to cure
The scornful injuries lowly hearts endure
From pampered Privilege? Thou art the core
Of Wisdom's social aim, who, all the more
Fierce Error threatens, toils to hold thee sure.
  On thy maternal bosom many a time
I lay my head, to dream that yet thy reign
In its completed influence every Clime
Shall sweeten; and as o'er some torrid plain
Fresh airs breathe vigor, quicken Man to gain
Capacity for Love's millennian prime.

NOTE This Sonnet was written to shew how lovingly essential are both social and religious charity to peace and good will amongst men – but written, at the same time, under a painful sense of the world-wide dearth of both. In the past and present of Time, how little of the former can we historically and currently point to. In the *now* of Man's spiritual abidance – in the book [of] life, the written immortality of mind, how utterly is the health of the latter shrunken up and poisoned by the hot and noxious breath of Sectarian intolerance! how is its mere literal form scorched and blasted by the fiery strife of creeds, called Christian! Insomuch is this the fact, that civil laws have to be revised, either to prevent its being expunged altogether from the page of human doings, or to compensate, supplementally, for its foregone insufficiency.

Alas! the active principles of all systematised Religions (old and new), purely natural religion excepted, do certainly and very manifestly assimilate to whatever is arrogant and exclusive in the dispositions of individual believers. They would absolutely appear from the whole stream of Church History, to be harmless only in the naturally impotent or the constitutionally indifferent. And they operate thus, I apprehend, because all Religions, besides the one above excepted, by fetching their sanctions directly from Heaven, do thereby preclude all philosophical benefit of doubt – the true course of true charity.

And it may be needful that I should here define the spirit of charity in its polemical significancy. It is a largeness and liberality of soul, disposing us to credit men of opposing opinions with honesty of motive, in the absence of positive proof to the contrary. It prepares us to feel and admit also, that it should not be assumed, that any differences of the kind, however wide, are sufficient to exclude them from the equal favor the Deity. It prepares us to admit further, that in all matters of pure speculation, it is quite possible that we ourselves may be wrong and they right who rest in opposite conclusions. And finally, whether such a possibility may be rationally grantable or not, it informs us, that God alone, at the tribunal of Heaven, is competent and authorised to execute judgement upon the issue.

Now a State Church, by royal adoption, (God's adoption being another thing), cannot be charitable out of the circle of its Articles, be they thirty-nine or ninety-nine; no more than a state nobility, by royal patent, (God's patent being another thing) can be humble and fraternal out of the precincts of a Court. So much for Anglican charity.

Neither can Presbyterianism, though republican in its form of government, be charitably disposed towards any other church system or spirit of Religion, being calvinistic in its doctrine. Fire and water; Calvinism and Charity; – are not these but equivalent extremes?

As to the Roman Church, it does not even pretend to the thing, otherwhere than amongst its Jesuitical outposts. Hate and Love; the Inquisition and Charity; – are not these too, but equivalent extremes?

That the end justifies the means is morally the most pernicious principle under heaven: (a directly opposite principle being the true one; namely, that the means justifies the end.) And yet all zealous religionists of every denomination act more or less under its influence. It has especially formed a part of the character of every bigoted Catholic whose dispositions and conduct I have had sufficient opportunities for watching and investigating: proceeding naturally enough from the blina[d]ly implicit belief in their Church's sole possession of the truth, in which that Church itself most zealously and jealously educates its children, or rather, its slaves. They are walled up by it through life from all benefit of doubt. And hence they conclude, (logically enough from such pernicious premises), that in subjecting any other religionist by any means, to its motherly supremacy, they are working such essential good in his behalf, as to preclude the very possibility of their doing him, at the same time, any essential harm. . .

I speak boldly. But every man has or should have his Mission in life; and mine is, I believe, to endeavour to brake away from the heart and mind of Man as many of its old-world fetters, as the intellectual insight of my nature, and the concurrency of my opportunities, may enable me to ascertain to be such, either absolutely or in effect: – in the first place, by the fearless promulgation of liberalizing and suggestive ideas; and in the next, by the doing of deeds correspondent to them, whenever and wherever the circumstances of the times shall so far concur with me as to make a fitting occasion. And with this conviction forever at my heart, why should I fear to speak out boldly and to the purpose? Nay, with a just occasion, could I call forth and modulate into articulate meaning even the firmamental thunders of God, I should neither fear nor hesitate to make *even* it a public medium for the utterance of any honest thought; – knowing well, and feeling unmistakeably, that Truth in the finality of things, has nothing to fear from honesty;and thus Truth and Intellectual Liberty, in their ultimate consequences, are inevitably included the the one in other.

The Great Fish of the Sea (See)

Your papist, in the Pope's infallibility,
Can see the only barrier of utility
   'Gainst anarchy, and heresy, and schism;
Whilst your grave churchman of the English nation
Beholds the source of popular salvation,
   Not in the Bible – but in the Catechism;
And thus for the same spiritual trout
Both angle, though with different tackle out:
A huge monopoly in the cure of souls,
High places, and blind worshippers in shoals.

Providential Design

Sense and passion, instinct, reason,
Time and tide, with every season:
The beasts that roam the grassy plain,
   The birds that ride the viewless air –
The flying cloud – the wind and rain –
   All rest; all motion; – all declare
   The Great Soul worketh everywhere.
And though the wilfulness of Man,
   May sometimes mar its just design,
The ultimately perfect Plan,
   Is none the less divine.

Note to Have Faith

As an implicit belief in God's goodness is the fountain head of all true religion, so a large faith in the capacity of human nature for good, is the root of all genuine morality. To think nobly of our original is to respect ourselves, and thence come chastity, honor and fortitude; while to believe it radically incapable and vile, is to live and die (speaking universally) on a level with this degrading estimate. It may be true – it *is* true, that man, the individual, is often desperately wicked. Communities also, may be mostly corrupt, selfish, unprincipled, and inhuman. Still the surviving sense of mankind, as to right and wrong, and glory and shame, is unfailingly just in the end. In the darkest ages – in the most vitious [vicious] societies, there have always sprung up a few faithful soldiers of God and Humanity, as ready to die as to live in the cause of Intellectual Liberty, which comprehends the interests of all Truth: and this proves sufficiently, that our capacities for good are primordiate and fundamental in the race; whereas our tendencies to evil, however obstinate and prevailing,

(Here the manuscript breaks off abruptly, the ensuing page has been either lost or misbound. (Ed.))

• ON SOCIAL AND SPIRITUAL ISSUES •

from The Witch of Hebron: A Rabbinical Legend

(The story thus far. A learned Rabbi is called to a sumptuous palace where the daughter of a friend is gravely ill. He discovers that her body is inhabited by a tormented spirit, who tells the Rabbi of his previous existence. Many lifetimes before the spirit sold his soul to the devil for a limited period of great power and wealth. At the expiration of this time he was saved from damnation by the intervention of an angelic shape, who offered him the possibility of salvation but who said he must do penance for his sins by undergoing a series of transmigrations commensurate to his faults. The spirit assumes in succession the forms of lion, eagle, and then of various women; and becomes aware of a gradual improvement in his physical and spiritual circumstances. Expiation is almost completed, and redemption apparently close at the beginning of Part VII, which describes his final rebirth and its consequences. (Ed.))

Part VII

'After some short and intermediate terms
Of transmigration – all in feminine forms,
And in the course of which through many ties
And kindly offices incurrred and done,
It seemed the temper of my spirit much
Had humanised; and in the last of which
'Twas mine, for once, to die a natural death:
Again I had some deep-down hold on being,
Dim as an oister's in its ocean-bed;
An aboriginal inception – yea,
A self-producing knot of living shoots
Which terminated all in one smooth surface,
From which branched forth tentacula, that searched
The darkling confines of my moist abode.
Then came a sense of free space, light and air,
And then of hunger, and along with this
Strong suctatorial powers. I could detect
Sweet food from sour, warm presences from cold,
And was beyond all doubt some sentient thing –
Some little vital centre, upon which
Much comfortable influence impinged,
But best I can recall, with what entire
Content I nestled betwixt two warm paps,
Each with its many-porous tap, both shaped
And colored both, – yea, to the very life,

Like two ripe mulberries of Palestine,
And from which, when I listed, without stint,
I drew a liquid that was meat and drink.
At length I could distinguish faces, forms,
And strove to imitate the sounds I heard;
Caught up the drift of speech, and knew at last
That all who came to see me and admire,
Called me Ben Bachai's daughter.

                         'Dark indeed,
But beautiful as a starry night I grew,
A Maid, the glory of her Father's house;
Her Mother's dovelet, filling all her wants
With tenderness and joy. Still as I grew,
By strange degrees the memory of all
That I had been came back upon my mind,
To fill it with wild sorrow and dismay:
To know I was a cheat, nor wholly what
I seemed even to my parents who did both
So doat upon me; that I was indeed
But half their daughter, and the rest a fiend,
With a fiend's destiny, – ah! this, I say,
Would smite me even in dreams with icy pangs
Of wordless woe – yea, even while I slept
So innocently, as it seemed, and so
Securely happy in the arms of Love!'

    As this was said, the Rabbi looked, and saw
That now again the Woman seemed to speak
As of herself, and not as heretofore
With moveless lips, and prisoned voice, that came
As from some dark duality within.
Her looks had changed too with the voice, and now
Again she lay – a Queen-like Creature, racked
With mortal sufferings, instant and extreme;
And who, when these grew tolerable at all,
Or for a time remitted, even thus
Went with her story on.

                    'At length upgrown
To womanhood, – on some mysterious pact
Obtaining 'twixt my Father's house and that
Of an Arabian Prince – time out of mind,
I was now wedded ere I wished; and he,

My husband, finally had come to claim
And bear me from my home – that happiest home
Which I should know no more: a Man most fair
To look upon, but void of force, – in truth,
The weakling of a worn-out line, who yet
(What merit in a Prince!) was not depraved,
Not wicked, not the mendicant of Lust,
And scoundrel slave of every selfish wish:
But mild, and even affectionate, even just.

   'My dowry was immense, and flushed with this
The Prince had summoned from his feudal tribe
Five hundred horse, all spearmen, to escort
And guard us Desert-ward. And as we went
These ever and anon, at signal given,
Would whirl around us like a thunder cloud,
Wind-torn, and shooting instant shafts of fire!
And thus we roamed about the Arabian wastes,
Pitching our camp amid the fairest spots.
Nor was this wandering life unpleasant. Oft
Under an awning, would I lay and gaze
Out at the cloudless ether where it wrapt
The silent mountains, like a conscious power
Big with the soul of an eternal Past.

   'But long this life might last not, for the Prince
Sickened and died – died poor; my dower as well
Having been squandered in our many jaunts
Upon the hungry horde that, day by day,
Was wont to prance about us: who ere long
Divining my extremity, grew loud
And urgent for rewards; – till, on a day,
By concert as it seemed, the tribe entire
Came fiercely round me, all demanding gifts,
Gifts that I had not – but in lieu of which
I was preparing to tongue-lash them well –
When, as this coil prest nearer – lo, I saw
Weaving his way amongst them, while they made
So soon as seen, with many signs of awe,
A lane for him to pass – the Bactrian Sage!
The Old Man of the Tombs! who soon came near,
And fixing me with his shrunk serpent eyes,
Waved off the abject Arabs, and then asked
"Why art thou poor? with needs so great upon thee

For wherewithal to glut yon greedy pack
Of Desert doggery? Again, behold,
I offer thee long life, and wealth, and power,
But on the same old terms."

      'Still vexed and chafed
I turned to him and said: Should I not know
By all the past, the nature of thy gifts
And what they lead to? – shows not substances,
Being evil, and thence non-essential all;
A vast accumulation of delusions
All terminating in eternal loss! –
"Well, take it as thou wilt," he said, "my gifts
Are not so weighed by all." And saying this
He went his way, while I retired within
My lonely tent to weep.

     'Next day the Tribe
Again assembled, to again enquire
What I designed to do. The poor they said,
No matter what their lineage might be,
Should pare their needs down to their shrunk estate:
That, if I wished it, being thus reduced,
An escort – say, a dozen spears or so –
Should see me safely to my Father's house.
This was too much! My blood arose, and I
Chode with them, calling them all things but men!
Dogs, jackals, monkeys! Go, I said, away
And see my face no more. Re-entering then
My tent, thus angered, – lo, there stood again
Within the twilight of its inner folds,
The withered Bactrian with his snaky eyes,
And wiry voice, that questioned as before:
"Why art thou poor? with needs so great upon thee,
And all this pretty baseness brattling round?
Am I not here to help thee? I, thy one
Sole friend – not empty, but with ample means.
– Behold the secrets of the mundane world!
There, down amongst the rock roots of the mountains,
What seest thou there? Look, as I point: even those
Strange miscreations, as to thee they seem,
Are the demoniac moilers that obey
Such arts as I possess: the gnomish brood
Of Demogorgan. See them how they moil

Amid those diamond shafts and reefs of gold
Embedded in the oldest drifts of Time,
And in the mire that was the first crude floor
And blind extension of the infant Earth:
Why art thou poor then, when such slaves as they
Might work for thee, and glut thy need with all
The matchless values which are there enwombed,
Serving thee always as they now serve me –
But on the old conditions. Nor are these
My servants only: turn thy looks aloft,
And watch the stars as they go swimming past!
Behold their vastness – each a world! Behold
Their brilliant populations, and the things
They trade in and converse with, such as Earth
May only in dim adumbrations show:
And these too, all shall be thy slaves," he said,
"As they are mine: upon the old conditions –
Even those thou erst didst swear to 'mid the Tombs."

   'But how, said I, might I make these obey me?
Straightway he took me by the hand, and said:
"Dost thou consent then to be mine for ever?"
I do consent, I said, – yet with a shudder
That shook me to the soul: and thereupon
He slipt a signet ring upon my finger:
Saying, "by this thou mayst command them all
To do thy bidding, in the earth beneath
And in the stellar heavens, with a sway
More absolute than was Solomon's of old."
– Suddenly then the desert winds arose
And blew with mighty stress amongst the tents;
Far off too in the east methought I heard
Low coming thunders: yea, a Storm was up!
For instantly aloft there ran a dread
Heart-killing turmoil, – and with this, behold
A mighty issue of miraculous light
Burst shaftwise forward, smiting Him in twain –
Yea, sheer in twain! and broken thus he fell,
Or so it seemed, down through the solid earth,
Leaving behind him on the blasted ground
A blue dent only, and a stench of fire!

'In vain I had shrunk into a dim recess,
For lo, once more, the Son of Paradise
Was lightning in my presence. Shame, remorse,
And misery unspeakable were mine,
As I at last dared to look up, and saw
Anger and sadness both upon his front.
At last he spake to me in tones that seemed
More gentle than I looked for or might hope:

"Couldst thou not rest content – all but redeemed,
All but re-born again – a Rabbi's daughter!
Enjoy as best thou may this ill-won power
Over the darker agencies of Time,
And bide the end – which end is punishment
But the more terrible the more delayed.
Yet know this also: thou shalt thus no more
Be punished in a body built of clay;
For Sammael must not triumph." Saying which
He vanished, leaving me abashed in soul,
And harrowed with ineffable regret:
And yet no power in heaven or hell, I said,
May now annul my deed: and therewith rose.

'Thus rich, twas mine to settle where I chose.
And long I was in finally choosing where:
Building vast Palaces in quiet view
Of ancient cities, or by famous streams,
I bought up beauty even as merchants buy
Their fabrics, in the markets of the world.
Men like to Gods were frequent in my halls,
And the most beautiful mothers earth could yield
Were nested in my chambers, brooding there
In downy privacy; like matron doves;
Whence come, as progeny, those Pages which
Thou seest at intervals glide in and out:
Beings so intensely beauteous that they look
Like striplings kidnapped from some skirt of heaven.
Yet sorrowful of countenance withal,
As knowing that their mortal doom is joined
With mine irrevocably; that with me
'Tis theirs to own these shows of Time; with me
To live, – with me to die.

'But all this pomp
Had no true taste of pleasure – no delight –
No satisfying end. And as 'tis said
A hunted roe will evermore beat round
Tow'rds whence he started first, I felt at length
Vehement longings for my native Hebron,
That spot in all the earth where I alone,
In tasting of it, had divined the worth
And sabbath quality of household peace.
Then coming hither, thus constrained, I pitched
My dwelling here, even this thou seest; built fair
And filled with splendors such as never yet
Under one roof-tree on this earth were stored.
See yon surpassing lustres! Could this Orb
Elaborate them? No. From Mars came that;
From Venus this. And yonder fiery mass
That looks as if 'twere breaking into flames
Of sun-bright glory – that from Mercury came.
Whence also came these viols, all instinct
With fervent music such as never yet
From earthly instruments might thrill abroad.'

Then siezing one of them, even as she spake
Over its chords she ran her ivory hand,
And instantly the Palace domes throughout
Rang resonant, as every hall and crypt
Were pulsing music from a thousand shells,
That still ran confluent with a mellow slide
And intercource of cadence: sweet and yet
Most mournful and most weird, and oft intoned
With a wild wilfulness of power that worked
For madness more than joy. 'Even such' she said,
'Were those delights with which I most conversed
In my so fatal loneliness of soul.

'Still all was show, not substance. All I held
But weighted more my ever-haunting fears
And apprehensions of a wrath to come,
From which no change of place, no earthly power,
Might shield me. Ah! I see it shadowing forth
Out of the foregone ages – forth with Fate,
Even like a coming night in whose dark folds
My soul shall ask to hide itself in vain!
In vain – in vain!'

           As thus the Woman spake,
Her brow grew dark, and suddenly she shrieked
In her great agony: 'O pray for me!
Pray Rabbi for the daughter of thy friend!
The hour is coming – nay, the hour has come!'
– There was a rustle as of wings aloft,
A sudden flicker in the lights below,
And she who until now seemed speaking, sank
Back on her pillow, and in silence there
Lay beautiful in the marble calm of death.
The Rabbi gazed on her, and thought the while
Of those far times when, as a girl, her grace
Had filled with pleasantness his old friend's house.
Then to her servants gave in charge the corpse,
And turning, left the chamber; through the vast
And echoing halls paced hastily, and thence
Out through the porch, and through the garden gate,
Much musing as he went. At length again
He turned to take a final view of what
Was now the House of Death. Can such things be?
All had evanished like an exhalation!
Only the woods that hung like clouds about
The steeps of Hebron, in the whitening dawn
Lay dark against the sky! Only a pool
Gleamed flat before him, where it seemed erewhile
The splendid structure had adorned the view!
Perplexed in mind, the Rabbi turned again
And hurried homeward, muttering as he went:
'Was it a Vision? Can such marvels be?
But what indeed are all things, even those
That seem most solid – Dust and Air at last!'

from Note to The Death of Shelley

NOTE I have written poems laudatory of Shelley, and to prevent my admiration of his poetical genius and character from being misinterpreted into evidence of a kindred atheism, and yet, at the same time, to vindicate the right he had, as a Man, not only to worship at whatever shrine he chose, but to advocate also whatever he believed true; I will venture some remarks on what I consider a proper liberty of speculative opinion. In advancing these, however, my object is not such much to reason men out of any belief whatever, as to reason them into a rational liberality of thought and conduct in respect to all those who may perchance differ from them, however widely.

To begin: I myself believe in the existence of a God, the one great Creator and providential Disposer of all things. Nothing, I apprehend, could shake me from this belief; but am I therefore to denounce the atheist, who in all social respects may be a better man than myself, – seeing that many so believing, according to the general notion, have been singular for the moral beauty and purity of their lives. By such a course, what do I more than instigate him in turn to denounce his denouncer, till between us, Charity, – that which should be 'all mankind's concern', is hunted from our homes. If it be a damnable sin to disavow any established or peculiar idea of the Deity, upon the disavower's own head be it at the tribunal of heaven, when Justice and Mercy and Truth are perfect – but not before any earthly one, where prejudice and cruelty and ignorance and error may be alone prevalent and alone powerful.

But what if such disavowal carry with it points of disbelief as to the God-ideas of every other man or set of men in the world? He should be left perfectly free notwithstanding either to believe or disbelieve, since he is fallible only in common with all other men; and openly to state and reason upon his convictions either way, so long as this be done in decent terms, and without personal intrusion. Out of blending contrariety harmony arises, and our moral differences should but constitute the moral music of life: for however individual Truth may be in its essence, it is manifold in its form; and hence to be comprehensively communicated with, it must be perceived through a variety of media answering to the different constitutions of men; – wherefore that knowledge were alone profoundly and universally applicable which should be a complete combination of the results of this perceptive multiformity.

Different men's perceptions of different particulars of Truth, or of more or less of it, will depend also, in a great degree, upon position and so forth. Thus several witnesses of any single occurence, supposing it to comprehend many details, may testify each of them to some certain circumstance, or momentary appearance, not mentioned or observed by another. But nevertheless the whole known truth of the occurrence in question, may reside in the narratives of each and all, when taken together, and arranged judiciously. Men therefore, to live in charity, must agree to differ; believing that in the finality of things, they only differ to agree. But why then should any care to make converts to their own peculiar views? But why not? So long as the mode and means employed be generous, open, and honest, it is well; because the endeavour to proselytise, in itself, is just the natural offspring of a sympathetic necessity, – and therefore the legitimate one.

* * *

• FROM NOTE TO THE DEATH OF SHELLEY •

A word in conclusion – Those unfraternal miscreants (the bigots of every denomination), who can rejoice in the belief that *their* religion, by the very fact of its saving *themselves*, must devote to the infernal gods the great majority of mankind, will no doubt bleat forth against the whole matter of this note, – and its author, their ancient war-cry of 'damnable'! But, than it, there is nothing more properly contemptible – nothing, except, indeed, the moral cowardice of those who, doubting its virtue, can yet be actively influenced by it. Ineffably contemptible it will be to all such at least, as have dared to conclude with the writer, under a lofty conviction of God's eternal wisdom and justice, that there can be no damnation for the righteous, be their creed whatsover it may. And for this last sentiment alone, I must submit to be pretty generally designated as a Free-thinker. But what of that? I already glory in the significance of such a title, and only regret that I am not more worthy of the moral liberty it implies. To slay Wrong with the sword of righteous words, and by the advocacy of a large and trustful spiritual freedom, to carry forward our entire race towards Perfection; – these are the God-appointed services of the modern soldiers of Truth; and whoever has done these, though but to the extent of liberalizing the mind and feelings of a single human being, has fought a good fight, and shall have earned a sure reward.

Life and Death

A little light, heat, motion, breath,
Then silence, darkness, and decay,
Are all that difference Life and Death
    In him that weareth clay:
But Time's *one drop* 'twixt that and this;
Ah! what a gulf of doom it is.

The cheek is fair, the eye is bold,
The ripe lip like a berry red:
Then the shroud clothes them; – thus behold
    The Living and the Dead!
And how Time's last cold drop serene
Swells to Eternity between!

Yet not for horror, nor to weep;
But through the solemn dark to see
That Life, though swift, is wonder-deep,
    And Death the only key,
That lets to that mysterious height
Where Earth and Heaven in God unite.

• ON SOCIAL AND SPIRITUAL ISSUES •

Happiness and Faith

No man, no woman, can be worldly happy!
Some flying cloud of infinite despair –
Some haggard sense of a blind destiny
Washing us weed-like out, we know not whither!
Some dread fore-influence like that which ruled
The emerald of Polycrites – will come
And overshadow us, when with those we love,
Even in the mornings of our surest joy!
For so it must be in a world like this,
With mortals conscious of mortality:
Conscious, though vaguely (and by reason most
Of some weird spell of that wild lore imposed
On credulous Fancy in her gipsy youth),
That Fortune, in her adamantine mould,
Casts all the forward intergrowths of time,
Uninfluenced by aught that would festoon
The random sprays, despite their first brute bent,
Into the bowers of a sequestered weal:
Conscious that Love, so mighty in itself,
So God-like, and thence capable to make
And keep the heart's integrity divine –
Yea, lift it through its pure intent to heaven,
Is yet how weak – weak as a brook-side reed,
When it would save from other hurt and loss,
From bodily decline, and sorrow, and death,
Its object! Something of all this must wring
Even the giddy in their gayest hour –
Must shudder at their hearts, and give their eyes
To see all Nature as in drear eclipse,
And all the lights of life burn dim, awhile,
Under the shadow of a swift despair –
Thought-swift, yet infinite, – infinite as the world,
And weirdly vague as the grey wraith of Time!
And hence the wisdom of a mind resolved
To wreak its every doubt on *one* belief,
That God is over and beholding all,
Approving virtue and contemning vice;
All which (as even the wise heathens held)
Is but the faith of reason; – while the heart
Goes farther, and can see in Him as well,
A God of Love, – a God delighting – yea,

Delighting father-like, in what the pure
Aspiring soul by deeds of truth projects
Through all the crass impediments of the world,
Out into higher being. Thus to will,
And in this will habitually to live,
Is through our dread-misgivings but to grow
As by recoils to higher ground, the more
Assured of final justice; and, if not
At heart healed wholly, yet resigned in thought
To all that hath befall'n or can befall.
Nay, if but lowly, we may even thus,
Though urged by doubt, from height to height ascend
Yet more and more into that central peace,
Which, overinforming the eternal world,
Comes thence (though only by the spirit felt)
Pulsating earthward through the starry dark,
Time's boundary, isling us in the Infinite:
Till all mysterious change – like objects seen
Updawning, out of the dead dark, – assumes
A morning promise, brightening into day;
And Death itself, so ugly to us once –
So frightfully final in its character
Of elemental frailty and decay, –
Puts on the likeness of a Living Soul
Stript of its mortal mask; – as Seraph wing'd!
There, in our prospect, with his beamy hand
Pointing a-head, and by the eloquent act
Hinting this doctrine to the heed of Faith:
Though life in time be wished, a fairer good
Awaits us, smiling at our human fears, –
Smiling awaits us, just beyond the grave.

The World and the Soul

Part I

From the crude records which mysterious Time
Hath graven on the crag-boned hills, and strewn
In crumbled fragments, and embedded deep,
On wild sea-shores, in dim dells, watery chasms,
And in the death-dark bowels of the Earth,
Where never sunshine, since Creation's dawn,

Hath fallen in its golden splendor down,
We learn that she, at dateless intervals,
Hath been the plastic and predestined mould
Of awfullest changes. And from these again, –
Reading their crude significance, more and more
Into coherency, – we wondering find
That her dark womb, through immemorial tracts
Of years so countless that they ghostly seem,
Hath also teemed with still successive births
Of vegetable prophecies of spirit,
Ever ascending to their own fulfilment;
And thence with sentient natures, linking on
In strict organic sequency, from forms
Of lowest power and purpose, – on and on,
To higher and highest.

      Thus her quickening mass
Quickened yet more, till knotted reptile things,
Stolid, yet frightful through mere multitude,
(Even as beheld *only in thought*), have swarmed
O'er all her clammy disc, as vile worms clothe,
In horrible mockery of both life and death
An else-stark corpse; – or beings unto which
The monstrous serpent of the Indian wastes
Were but a minim, in her miry lap
Have wallowed, snorting in their ponderous joy –
Beings enormous! but in function low,
And gross in shape – yea, ugly as enorm!
And evermore pre-doomed to perish, when
Her altering surface grew the meet abode
For things of greater beauty. Whether wrought
Into such meetness by set laws of change,
For ever active, and thence through all time
Distributing their forces; or by some
Mystical energy at work within,
Of Demogorgon kind; or by the sweep
Of sudden cataclysms wild and vast;
Or by the upburst of internal fires,
Instant and universal!

      First emerged
Mountains abrupt, like those upon the moon,
Scarred through with fissures out of which there seethed
A white volcanic heat; while spongy growths

Of cypress-dark and flowerless forests, filled
Vast valleys with a damp and noisome shade,
But luminous at intervals with drear
Avernian lakes, that blackened under storms
Drifting aloft, or imaged back the bulk
Of bat-like monsters, flying o'er; or glassed
(Along their low shores shadowing out) the huge
Unwieldy masses of some mammoth herd,
As into the dim spaces of the dense
And bordering woods it passed, and onward then
Crashed, munching as it went. And yet on this
So lonesome scene, the sun arose as now,
True to his season, and the moon unveiled
Her pale face over it night after night,
Bevied about with all her golden train
Of stellar glories raying influence down.
Yea thus, for countless centuries, beneath
The fulgent host of heaven, did all the bare
And slopeless hills show ghastly in their light,
And the dull waters gleam: although as yet,
Through all these patient periods immature,
No soul intelligent, save God himself,
Might know or visit them –

     But lo, at last,
In jubilant ascension, Man, and all
The tribes of living creatures over which
He reigneth absolute, with comelier forms
Of higher cast, and inwardly endued
With spirits and faculties that flourished forth
To finer issues and to ends more nice,
Gave to their mother Earth's time-tempered orb
That worth and excellence which now are hers.

 Then, on the hills, the hunter's voice went forth,
And, in the valleys, the glad chaunt of birds
Chimed sweetly with the gurgling interflows,
And musical motions, manifold and mixt,
Of rivers in their broad abundant flow
Through boundless depths of bloomy boughs, all tossed
And billowing in the breeze; and Echoes, housed
In rocky steeps, and caves, and twilight dells,
Made merry with the cheerful noise that came
Mellowed by distance, out of lowing glens

And multitudinously bleating vales,
In large scopes, – lying all within each broad
Allotted heritage that stretched around
The low-roofed homesteads of an early world; –
Low-roofed, but staunch, – and welcome – fraught, as seen
Bosomed in trees from which ripe golden globes
Hung clustered, while about them rippled deep
Glad fields of rustling corn: till hence at length,
Through all meet channels working, Nature taught
Music to Art; and answering to a want
Hence too created, Poetry arose
Out of the dayspring like a morning star
Upon the awakened spirit of delight;
And thence descending in her influence, grew
More intimate and plastic, – till at last
Semblance idealised in hues, or wrought
From the rude rock into a life which spake
The language of immutable Loveliness,
Adorned the abodes of Learning, and the shrines
Of Worship, and of Virtue; – Sister Arts,
Three Sister Arts in fellowship divine –
A triune glory of exalted *Soul*.

Part II

But dare we think the awful laws of Change
From good to better, still, though over roads
So rough in seeming have even yet an end?
That Earth is Man's for ever? His and theirs,
The tribes o'er which pre-eminent he reigns
As king – his one true Kingship? No: the Hours
That shall behold her the prepared abode
For new successions in the Scheme of Life,
May even *now* – like a long flight of storks
Or ere it loom in view, – up, where the waves
Of ocean welter in the spectral haze
On heaven's apparent verge; – thus, even *now*,
May these upon their dim but destined way
Be winging world-ward, through the eternal clouds
That hide the Future in their pregnant folds.

But, granting this, from whence, it may be asked,
Might spring these novel Orders? Even from where
All that preceded them in time's long tract
Have hitherto sprang life-ward: – from the womb
Prolific of that Spirit of the World
Called Nature, and wherein, even from the first,
In virtual preparation shall have slept
Their causes, – darkling; but awaiting so
The evoking word of God! And what besides
Were needed, for thrice greater things, – the births
Of mightiest Systems, than that potent Word
Which the mind heareth, as expressed through laws
Whose sure results are but the far-produced
Decisions of His will, – as fore-designed,
Will and design in an omnicient Spirit
Being co-incident.

    Or rather, what
I would adumbrate in this serious song,
Were but progressive changes in the sum
And complement of that Divine Idea
Whereof the Earth's so solid-seeming mass
Is, with its fleshly populations whole,
The vesture, – yea, the tactual shape, and thence
The visual sign in manifold reflection,
As ever forth fulfilling, more and more,
Its part in that great Sequence which ensures
The prospering intercourse of all the worlds:
Even as a human thought – so far as what
Is finite, and imperfect therefore, may
With Infinite compare, – as knowledge grows
Before it, and combines all congruent things,
A Necessary progress undergoes
In its accruing unity with Truth.

 But come what changes may, yet is the Soul,
As individualised in all mankind,
Beyond the swoop of chance, and lifted high
Out of the wasting whirl of brute Appearance,
When thence eliminated. She, complete

In her self-being, evermore aspires
An ultimate of all that went before –
A Spirit of Thought, and thence of that prime Cause
Whereby the world itself began and is.
And thus derived, – a Virtue purer far
Than that invisible ethereal fire –
That vital spirit of the world which breathes
Through Being's boundless lungs, she cannot know
Or darkness, or corruption; but must be
A missioned Liberty, and thence endued
With powers of self-development, that break
All bondage! Yea, ancestrally a spark
From God's own brightness, goes she world-ward forth
To die not, but to clothe for evermore
Her mighty life and wondrous faculties
In robes of beauty and of use, and all
The comforting integuments which sense
Weaves for her wearing, in the loom of Time,
Out of the hoards and harvests of the earth;
And thence by transmigration made through that
New birth called Death, in the adopted worth
And garniture of many *or all* of those
Innumerable orbs, that spangle thick
The neighboring heaven with seats of being, – such
As host on host yet farther forth, enrich
Infinite spaces, populous alike
With kindred glories bosomed all in Him!
As being indeed the million-featured modes
Of His omniscient Power; – each several mode
A shining link in *one* eternal chain
Of progress – to Perfection.

                       Here we rest
Secure in soul. In secular safety too,
Here rest we, – satisfied; that come what may
Of change to Earth herself, or unto those
Her kindred glories that compose so bright
A Sisterhood in heaven, – though such as yet
Shall beat them into ruin and involve
Their death *in seeming*; still, in sure reserve,
For each some restoration must abide
In the unfailing consciousness of God,
And that divine necessity which makes
Creation and Advancement evermore

Link onward through all being: wherefore She,
And They, though after some dread shock of change
Long lying shrouded, shall again awake,
And yet again, – wake jubilant, to hear
His far-off trumpet through the dark of doom
Calling them up into a state yet more
Exalted, as yet nearer to his own
Internal excellence and central peace.

Note to the poem called Geologia

Of course it is not insinuated in this Poem, that the starry systems of the Universe, in their infinitude, are the Mind of God itself, but only that they are the reflected thoughts of its divine intelligence in the boundless and eternal development of a necessary though not *necessitated* progress towards perfection. And when the orbit of this our Earth, to instance it individually, (now an elipse) shall have become a circle, towards which it is obviously tending, its temperature, – in fact, its whole physical constitution perhaps, in relation to sentient being, will be thereby perfected in perpetuity, – to continue so thenceforward, as eternally consummated in the mind of the Creator. But the Divine Intelligence, not only conceives and interpenetrates, but is also superior and external to these starry systems: as a human intelligence not only gives birth and fashion to its own peculiar thoughts, but is also independently existent. They are not *it*, though they are of it. In other words, though they proceed from it, they do not constitute it.

And as the mind of man has power to comprehend these reflexional systems of the universe, which cannot otherwise comprehend themselves (leaving out of the question their own inhabitative intelligences), it must be something which in its nature is different from them – must, in fact, be an offspring having absolute kindred with the Divine Mind itself, however much lower in degree [,] in relation to the Infinite [,] the Finite may declare it to be. However dependent then upon the Deity, as its parent, it has yet a *self*, is spiritually distinct, is immutably entire within this Self, and therefore immortal.

On the other hand, the material things of the Universe are purely attributive to the mind of God, as thoughts: but thus proceeding, however progressively mutable, they must yet be eternal. Our thoughts in their finite degree are likewise enduring, though likewise subject to progressive mutation. It is the media – the material symbols through which the human mind expresses its conceptions that alone are perishable (so to speak). Were these of a like essence, our manifested thoughts would be as indestructibly visible as the vast stars of night. Nay, this may be said to be almost the fact as it is: I mean in those cases in which from their sympathetic mastery, as the fruits of Genius, they have been committed to some perpetuating channel of communication like the Press. In reading Shakespeare, for instance, can we confound his glorious ideas with the mere print and paper of his book or even with the sounds which are therein symbolised. True, these are instinct with them, are the media of their revelation, but they themselves exist by virtue of a native spirituality in union with Truth, as emanations of an immortal intelligence, itself the personal offspring of an eternal one – the intelligence of God: the distinction here between an immortal and an eternal Intelligence being, that the first is *immortal* when once in distinct existence, the latter *eternal* as having always been.

The Silence of Faith

A thousand million souls arise
   Out of the cradle of To-day,
And, like a storm, beneath the skies
   Go thundering on their destined way!
     But ere To-morrow's sun
     His ancient round hath run,
   The storm is past – and Where are they?
Is asked of Faith by pale Dismay:
     O say,
     Where – where are they?
And faith – even Faith herself, hath not a word to say.
   With her serene assurance thrown,
   Like moonlight, into the Unknown,
   And all her clasping tendrils curled
About the steadfast pillars of the never-failing world,
   To that wild question of Dismay
   – Yet hath she not a word to say:
   And only lifts her patient eyes
     Up from earth's tempest-trampled sod,
   To fix them, – out in the eternal skies, –
     On all she knoweth – God.

•4• On Nature and Human Response

Life Without and Within

How vain seems life, how worthless, when we scan
Its outside only – and we laugh at Man!
But when we pore into its depths, we see
An awful import in its mystery:
For what is deep is holy, and must tend
To some divinely universal end.

A Similitude

Downward, through the bloomy roofage
   Of a lonely forest bower,
Come the yellow sunbeams, – falling
   Like a burning shower:
So through heaven's starry cieling
   To the hermit soul's abode,
Comes the Holy Spirit, – earthward
   Raying down from God.

A Flight of Wild Ducks

Far up the River – hark! 'tis the loud shock
Deadened by distance, of some Fowler's gun:
And as into the stillness of the scene
It wastes now with a dull vibratory boom,
Look where, fast widening up at either end
Out of the sinuous valley of the waters,

And o'er the intervenient forest, – up
Against the open heaven, a long dark *line*
Comes hitherward stretching – a vast Flight of Ducks!
Following the windings of the vale, and still
Enlarging lengthwise, and in places too
Oft breaking into solitary dots,
How swiftly onwards comes it – till at length,
The River, reaching through a group of hills,
Off leads it, – out of sight. But not for long:
For, wheeling ever with the water's course,
Here into sudden view it comes again
Sweeping and swarming round the nearest point!
And first now, a swift airy rush is heard
Approaching momently; – then all at once
There passes a keen-cutting, gusty tumult
Of strenuous pinions, with a streaming mass
Of instantaneous skiey streaks; each streak
Evolving with a lateral flirt, and thence
Entangling as it were, – so rapidly
A thousand wings outpointingly dispread
In passing tiers, seem, looked at from beneath,
With rushing intermixtures to involve
Each other as they beat. Thus seen o'erhead
Even while we speak – ere we have spoken, – lo!
The living cloud is onward many a rood,
Tracking as 'twere in the smooth stream below
The multifarious shadow of itself.
Far coming – present – and far gone at once!
The senses vainly struggle to retain
The impression of an Image (as the same)
So swift and manifold: For now again
A long dark *line* upon the utmost verge
Of the horizon, steeping still, it sinks
At length into the landscape; where yet seen
Though dimly, with a wide and scattering sweep
It fetches eastward, and in column so
Dapples along the steep face of the ridge
There banking the turned River. Now it drops
Below the fringing oaks – but to arise
Once more, with a quick circling gleam, as touched
By the slant sunshine, and then disappear
As instantaneously, – there settling down
Upon the reedy bosom of the water.

A Summer Night Scene

Let us go forth: for beautiful is the night!
Most beautiful! The wide fields deep in maize,
And orchard-bosomed homes, and, zoning all,
   The old and solemn woods
   Float in a silver sea,
Poured from the fountains of the rising Moon,
Who, half behind yon hill-top, seemeth there
   A casque of figured gold
   On Earth's uplifted head.
   (Hertha's lifted head)

Heaven's sparkling companies have clustered out
To hail their coming Queen, and interweave
Their fervent peans with her milder strain;
   But over all beneath
   Reigns Silence, – undisturbed
Save when, at solemn intervals, there hangs
Within the viewless tresses of the breeze,
   Some accent of the brook
   Quick glittering from afar.

The Spouse of Infinitude

Behold, the Moon is in the midst of heaven,
Serenely shining, – like a giant pearl
Amongst the fierier jewell'ry of Night,
Infinitude's dark Spouse; – dark, but no less
With inconsumable and boundless beauty,
And loveliness – the lovelier because
Of its unfathomable mystery –
Arrayed as with a robe. And who can look
Upon her dusk but so resplendent face,
And thus, unfailing recurrent, she
Comes over in her fellowship with Time,
Nor feel that she was nourished into being
Upon the bosom of Almighty Power
Illimitably active, and in strict
Coincidence with Eternal Verity?
And thence with Goodness? Yea, for what indeed

Is Truth itself, as in the light of thought
We see it purging all things into means
For purer issues, but the final test
And crowning evidence of Deific Love?

Note to the poem Early Summer (beginning 'Chasing cold Winter's dull sadness')

The first two were the spontaneous overflowings of that uncontainable gladness with which, in early youth, the coming of Summer always inspired me. In my boyhood, I particularly remember, that my very life at such seasons was a plastic centre as it were for all that was exhilerating in surrounding nature – the fountain-home of a thousand currents of joy, bright and gushing as the mountain rills, fresh and pleasant as the breath of heaven. And should not a sensibility to the large and beautiful beneficences of the outward universe, be promoted as much as possible in all, not merely as a medium of healthy pleasure, but also as one of the strongholds of rational religion? (I would have said *natural* religion had I not wished to imply more.) But to answer the question: I think it should. For though from an instinctive fear of degenerating into cant, God as their author may not be directly referred to in our expression of the delight of which they are the ministers; still in the very secret of the heart's gladness there resides an acknowledgement of his bounty; because the Beautiful and the Good are ultimately traceable to that source alone. To *feel* the one is to *admit* the consequence, however tacitly; and to become conscious, even thus mediately, of the Divine Presence, is to become better. – The following verses are another result of the same overflowing sense of vernal delight which prompted those above noted, when considerably sobered down saddened by the hard experiences of Manhood (A lesson from Nature).

Early Summer

'Tis the early Summer season
   When the skies are clear and blue, –
When wide warm fields are glad with corn
   As green as ever grew,
And upland growths of wattles
   Engolden all the view.

O there is a conscious joyance
  In a heaven so clearly blue!
And it must be a *felt* happiness
  That thus comes blooming through
Great Nature's mother-heart when
  The golden year is new!

When the woods are whitened over
  By the jolly cockatoo,
Or swarm with birds as beautiful
  As ever gladdened through
The shining hours of Time when
  The golden year was new.

A Mid-Summer Noon in the Australian Forest

Not a bird disturbs the air,
There is quiet everywhere;
Over plains and over woods
What a mighty stilness broods.

  Even the grasshoppers keep
Where the coolest shadows sleep;
Even the busy ants are found
Resting in their pebbled mound;
Even the locust clingeth now
In silence to the barky bough:
And over hills and over plains
Quiet, vast and slumbrous, reigns.

Only there's a drowsy humming
From yon warm lagoon slow coming:
'Tis the dragon-hornet – see!
All bedaubed resplendently
With yellow on a tawny ground –
Each rich spot nor square nor round,
But rudely heart-shaped, as it were
The blurred and hasty impress there,
Of a vermiel-crusted seal
Dusted o'er with golden meal:
Only there's a droning where
Yon bright beetle gleams the air –
Gleams it in its droning flight
With a slanting track of light,
Till rising in the sunshine higher,
Its shards flame out like gems on fire.

Every other thing is still,
Save the ever wakeful rill,
Whose cool murmur only throws
A cooler comfort round Repose;
Or some ripple in the sea
Of leafy boughs, where, lazily,
Tired Summer, in her forest bower
Turning with the noontide hour,
Heaves a slumbrous breath, ere she
Once more slumbers peacefully.

O 'tis easeful here to lie
Hidden from Noon's scorching eye,
In this grassy cool recess
Musing thus of Quietness.

Dawn in the Australian Forest

It is the Morning Star, arising slow
Out of yon hill's dark bulk, as she were born
Of its desire for day; then glides she forth
And up into the dim sky, leaving still
A whiteness in her wake that whitens more
As she ascends, till all the gloomy woods
Are touched along their multiformous lines
By a faint gleaming azure, that instils,
With a soft clarifying sequence, down
Through their dense fleeces of dark-heaping leaves,
As out beyond them, from the horizon, now,
The dayspring strengthens momently, and spreads
Into the mightier Morn.

      Meanwhile the stars,
Those golden children of Eternity,
From its eclipsive growth have all withdrawn
Within the Unapparent. Stronglier still,
Though with a gradual increment, works out
And downward, even to the grassy ground,
That skiey gleam and azure prevalence
Which first bespake the Dawn: till all the trees
Eastward disposed, - against the brightening sky
Clearly defined to their minutest sprays, -
Stand in unspeakable beauty. Moist with dew,
And glinting all with a dim silveriness,
The leaves curve out or tremblingly depend
From the remoter tracery of the boughs,
While interfused through all, the clearing light
Keeps steeping all in a diviner glow -
Diviner every moment; - for beyond
The ruddy cheek of Morning more and more
Is breaking into smiles, to fill the world
To overflowing with the joy of Light!
And the great soul of Man with a relief
Surpassing joy, as thereby given afresh
To feel the presence of that greater Soul
Which makes all Nature, and of which itself
Is but an effluence, however far
Projected, or detached by tract of time;
Even as a sunbeam's fountain is the sun,

Whether it hit the earth, or glance away
Into infinitude, – shooting on for ever.

Names of Colonial Birds

Never were God's creatures named – or rather nicknamed – after a more barbarous fashion than were our native birds by the first comers. Take for example the following string of names: – there are Old Soldiers, Bald-headed Friars, Leather Bellies, Native Companions, Laughing Jackasses, Doctor Faustuses, Gorgers, Cocktails, Bobtails, and Governor Fovaus. Of the last name, however, it may be remarked, that no two sounds could more closely resemble the notes of the bird so-called – and *it* therefore may be allowed to pass; especially as it is likely that this resemblance was first detected during Colonel Fovaux's administration of the Government. 'Native Companion,' too, may have been bestowed by some one having a grain of ideality of the John Bunyan vein – but for the others! they 'fright the *Muse* from her propriety.' and indeed are only fit to conjure with, like the names of Glendower's devils. Yet for the sake of a passing joke, let us even try how they will serve in rhyme:

Morning

With purple-tinct fingers, Aurora is drawing
   The bed-curtains now of the jolly-faced Day,
While in yon old ironbark, loudly jawing,
   Are two Laughing Jackasses – jawing away.

Beautiful change hath inspired the creation!
   Bobtails and Cocktails are loud in the brier:
In the gum tree the Gorger pours forth his oration,
   And below in the wattle, the Bald-headed Friar.

Old Soldiers are piping in every thicket,
   In flocks Leather Bellies come chattering by;
And see – Doctor Faustus! that conjurer wicked,
   Is getting well-trounced by a testy old Pie!

Long-legged Native Companions are freaking,
   At times in the blady-grass patches below;
And from tree top to tree top, a hawk there is sneaking
   (As some land-griper used) after Governor Fovaux.

But seriously, these vile names should be dropped as soon as possible – and indeed are being dropped – or rather, they are dying off with the old hands. At present, in some of the remote districts, first penetrated by intelligent Squatters, the birds (and most other things) are allowed to retain their aboriginal names, which are generally very beautiful. This is just as it should be, and is indicative moreover of the prevalence of good taste – a thing always, and in all places, worthy of commendation.

The Scenic Part of Poetry

A young critic of great promise has written: 'Who shall compute how much excellent versification has been squandered on what is called "descriptive poetry," in forgetfulness, rather than ignorance of a cardinal truth – that physical nature *beautiful* to celestial spirits, perhaps also in a modified sense of the word, to the lower brute creation in this world of ours, is *only poetical* in its immediate relation to the inner life and spirit of man'. Now this must be taken with great limitation. It would otherwise sweep away at least two-thirds of Wordsworth, and leave us scarcely a leaf of the 'Seasons' of Thomson. But the truth is, *beautiful nature* is *poetical*, not only in its immediate, but in its whole relation to man – and further *in itself*, simply because it cannot be *unrelated* to man. As the mere richly wrought framework of his picture, (so to speak) it is *poetical* – even without the actual presence of the picture, though more so with it. It is in this region that Poetry and Painting more particularly conjoin, as Poetry and Music do in the measures and modulations of verse. What natural beauty may be in the abstract – unrelated to man – is a matter wholly foreign to the present disquisition; as it is one perhaps that is wholly without the pale of all useful enquiry. Had our young friend written – 'only poetical *in the highest sense*, &c.,' he would have been quite right. The whole canon with regard to what is poetical, includes all things that are beautiful and sublime: these, impassioned or idealised, though by contemplation only, are always and inevitably poetical, whether in immediate or remote relation to man, though the more intensely so, the nearer this relation.

A Coast View

High 'mid the shelves of a grey Cliff, that yet
Hangeth in bluffs enormously above,
In a benched cleft, as in the mouldered chair
Of grey-beard Time himself, I sit alone,
And gaze with a keen wondering happiness
Out o'er the Sea. Immensely rolling forth,
See how it stretches to the circling bend
That verges Heaven: – a vast luminous plain
Of waters, changeful as a lover's dream!
Into great spaces mapped by light and shade
In constant interchange, or under clouds
The billows darken, or they simmer bright
In sunny scopes of measureless expanse!
'Tis Ocean dreamless of a stormy hour,
Calm, or but gently heaving; – yet, O God!
What a blind fate-like mightiness lies coiled
In slumber, under that wide-shining face!
While, o'er the watery gleam, – there where its edge
Banks the dim vacancy, the topmost sails
Of some tall Ship whose hull is yet unseen,
Hang as if clinging to a cloud that still
Comes rising with them from the void beyond,
And bellying over – like a heavenly net
Drawn slowly upward by ethereal hands.

   And if I look aloft, how deep the sky
That arches Ocean! – deeper far, it seems,
Than elsewhere. See how delicately rare
Are those sky colors that keep flickering up
From the remote horizon! Beautiful
Those lucid traceries of woven cloud
That float about the sun; and lustrous too
Are the white masses overhead, that move
And gather inland tow'rds the verdant hills.

• A COAST VIEW •

   Withdrawing now the eye from heaven, behold
The Coast how wonderful. Proportions strange,
And unimaginable forms, more quaint,
More wild and wayward than were ever dreamt
By a mad architect, keeping crowding out
As runs the eye along it. Semblances
Of pyramidic structures vague and rent,

   Withdrawing now the eye from heaven, behold
The Coast how wonderful. Proportions strange,
And unimaginable forms, more quaint,
More wild and wayward than were ever dreamt
By a mad architect, keeping crowding out
As runs the eye along it. Semblances
Of pyramidic structures vague and rent,
Hunch ledging stairwise from the general range,
Or dark time-wasted columns, leaning out
Under the bluffs, and in their seeming such
As old Assyrian trowels might have reared,
Support fantastic arches. Rugged domes,
And minarets in ruin, freak the sides
Of chasms spann'd by crude and haggard bridges;
Or overhanging Cliffs like this whose shelf
Sustains me, rest on buttresses of more
Than Babylonian vastness; – while below
Against their bases everlastingly
Beats the white wrath of the relentless surge.

   Yet even amid these rugged forms the warm
And gentle ministry of Spring hath wrought
Its work of love. Most sparingly indeed,
But thence most gratefully, a nameless shrub
With flame-bright blossom, tufts each guttered ledge
That holds a scanty soil; and rarer still,
Green runners from some sheltering crevice throw
Their tendrils o'er the shelves, and trailing thence
Touch the stern faces of the rocks with beauty.

Nor wants the scene its meet inhabitants.
Below the porpoise breaches, and the crab
Waits for his prey amid the wave-washed stones
That glisten to the sun, – gleaming himself
Whene'er he moves, as if his wetted shell
Were breaking into flames; or more remote,
Out in the watery spaces may be seen
Some solitary diver's shining back.
Sea gulls go clanging by, and overhead
Sits the white-breasted hawk, with many a sleek
And silver pinioned wanderer in the winds
That forrow the great visage of the Deep,
And who, in conjugal convention met,
Hoard here their mottled eggs and rear their young
Amid the jags and fissures of the crags.

How nourishing is Nature to the soul
That loves her well! not only as she acts
In instant contact with its quickened powers,
But as she tempers all its after-moods
Through distant memories and remotest tokens.
And hence, when thus beloved, not only here
By the great Sea, or amid forests wild,
Or pastures luminous with lakes, is she
A genial Ministress; – but everywhere!
Whatever testifies of her is good,
However common; fresh, however known.
Dead city walls may pen us in, but still
Her influence seeks to find us, – even there,
Through many a simple means. A vagrant mass
Of sunshine, falling into some void place,
Shall warm us to the heart, and trade awhile,
Though through some sorrowful reminiscence,
With instincts which, regenerated thus,
Make us child-happy. A stray gust of wind,
Pent in and wasting up the narrow lanes,
Shall breathe insinuations to our age
Of youth's fresh promise. Even a bird, though caged,
Shall represent past freedom, and its notes
Be spirited with memories that call
Around us the fresh fumes of bubbling brooks
And far wild woods. Nay, even a scanty vine,
Trailing along some backyard wall, shall speak
Love's first green language; and (so cheap is truth)

A bucket of clear water from the well
Be in its homely brightness beautiful.

The Bush Fire

Part I

'Tis nine o'Clock – to bed! cried Egremont,
Who, with his youthful household, long ago,
(The sturdy Father of seven sturdy boys)
Dwelt in a lone home nested far within
Our virgin Forest, that scar[c]e broken then,
As with an unshorn fleece of gloomy wood
Robed the vast bulk of all the mighty Isle.
But ere retiring finally, he went
Forth as his wont was to survey the night.

   'Twas clear and silent: and the stirless woods
Seemed dreaming in the witch-light of the Moon,
As like a boat of stainéd pearl, she rode
Dipping, as 'twere, with a propendent motion
Amid the ridges of a wavy cloud –
The only cloud in heaven: round which afar,
The larger stars out of the depths of space
Swelled pendulous, trembling with a glow globose –
So keenly clear the night. And while our Friend
Looked thus observingly abroad, he marked
All round him, listing the horizon's verge,
Save where against the starry aether, one
Enormous ridge drew its black line along,
A broad unusual upward glaring gleam –
Such a drear radiance as the setting sun
Effuses when the atmosphere is stormy.

   Nor long was he in doubt whence this arose –
Divining soon the cause – a vast Bush Fire!
But deeming it too distant yet for harm,
During the night betiding, to repose
With his bed-faring household he retired.

Sound was their sleep: for honesty of life
Is somewhat lumpish when 'tis once a-bed.
And now the darkness of the night was past:
When, with the dreams of Egremont, a strange
And momently approaching roar began
To mingle, and insinuate through them more
And more of its own import – till a Fire
Huge in imagination as the world
Was there sole theme: then, as arising wild,
His spirit fled before its visioned fear,
He started from his sleep, – to find indeed
The hardly (it seemed) exaggerated type's
Conflagrant hugeness from abroad derived
In warning! For what else, however terrible,
Save Ocean snoring to a midnight storm,
Might breathe with a vitality at once
So universal, so immense, and fierce,
As that which now reigned roaringly without.

Up leaping from his couch, scarce did he wait
To clothe himself, ere forth he rushed, – and, lo,
Within the circling forest he beheld
A vast and billowy belt of writhing fire,
That shed a wild and lurid splendor up
Against the whitening dawn, come raging on!
Raging and roaring as with ten thousand tongues
That prophesied destruction! On it came!
Devouring with a lapping hungriness
Whatever shrivelled in its scorching breath –
A dreadful Apparition! such as Fear
Concieves when dreaming of the front of Hell.

No time was there to lose. 'Up – up!' he cried,
To all the house. Instantly all within
Was haste and wonder, and in briefest space
The whole roused family was staring out
In speechless admiration! Yea, in that
Wild sympathetic union with the Terrible,
Which in the sudden and unlooked for midst
Of a tremendous danger, oft ensues,
And, for a time, even through its own extreme,
Keeps terror dormant! But more urgently,
The voice of Egremont again was heard:
'Lose not a moment! Follow me at once!

Each with whatever he can grasp of use,
And carry unincumbered as he flies!'

   Out from the doorway, right before them, – lo,
A narrow strip of clearing, like a glade,
Stretched on tow'rds a bald summit. Thitherward
Our perilled people now were hurrying all;
While in their front, beneath the ridge, a dense
Extent of brushwood into which the Fire's
Bright teeth were ravening, – near, and nearer, brought
The rapid danger! Shall they reach that hill
Unscathed, their only refuge? Well they speed
Past the red-rushing fronts of fire! and see,
As thus they hurry on, how more and more
Disclosing spectre-like from the red gloom
And brushing through them with long whizzing bounds,
The kangaroos string forth in Indian file
Across that strip of clear; with here and there
A wild dog slinking rapidly along
Amid the general rout, human and brute!
And all, *for once*, unharried as they go
By those keen foes of theirs, the household dogs,
That whining hang upon their masters' flight
As it strains onward, so bewildered seem they! –
Thus passingly involved, yet pauseless rush
Our people – urged into a desperate pace
By the hot glare that now comes sweltering round,
And the loud roar that loudens all along
The line of their wild flight, as if the flames
Were wrathful at their prospect of escape,
And hurried also – hurried with a swoop,
And raged more ruinously while they weaned
To intercept, and blast them! But at length,
The brush-bald border of the summit's gained,
Even as the Fire, upon the left hand, breaks
Against the hill's base like a ruddy surge;
And halting, they look back – in safety all,
Though scorched and blistered by the cinders, blown
Like burning sleet against them as they ran.

   But see, no sooner had they crowding passed
Out from the brush, where into a broad dell
It dipped on all hands round a sullen pool,
And where the rank and withered runners lay

In tangled heaps, – than a vast swath of flame
Lifted and hurried forward by the wind
Over their very passage-track, was pitched
Sheer into it, with a loud thud like thunder!
Which such a thud as the sea-swell gives up
From under the ledges of some hanging cliff;
And, in an instant, all the wide sere depth
Was as a lake of Hell! and hark! as then,
Even like a ghastly pyramid the mass
Of surging flames, inlapping as they rose,
And welding as it were all into one
Dense pile, rushed lancing up – up with them still
A long mad shriek of mortal agony went
Writhing aloft! – so terrible indeed,
That those who heard it, never until then,
Might deem a voice so earnest in its fear,
So strenuous in its anguish, could have being
In the live bosom of the suffering world!
But soon did they divine, even to their loss,
Its import; – there a giant Steed, their best,
Had taken cover, and had perished so.

Part II

Tented with heaven only, but all grouped
In safety now upon that hill's bare top,
Egremont and his household looked abroad
Astonished at the terrors of the time!
Down sunk their roof-tree in the fiery surge:
Which entering next a high-grassed bottom, thick
With axe-ringed trees all standing bleak and leafless,
Tenfold more terrible in its ravage grew –
Upclimbing to their tops! And soon, as when
Upon some day of national festival,
From the tall spars of the ship-crowded port,
Innumerous flags, in one direction all,
Tongue outward, writhing in the wind; even so
From those dry boles where still the did [dead] bark clings,
Hanging in ragged strips half shelled away,
And from their intermingled mass above
Of withered boughs, myriads of flaming tongues
Lick upward, or aloft in narrowing flakes
Stream quivering out upon the tortured blast –
Quivering and flapping and commiting all
Into one wide and multifarious blaze!

• THE BUSH FIRE •

   Scared ever onward, in successive starts,
By the fast following roaring of the Fire,
A flight of parrots o'er the upper ridge
Comes whizzing, and then circling low, alights
In a gay colored crowd amid the oaks
That skirt as with a feathery fringe the base
Of yon steep terrace – being, as it seems,
Deterred from still proceeding by the smoke
Uprolled in front, heap ridging over heap,
Like a dim moving range of spectral mountains.
There they abide, and listen in their fear
To the tremendous riot of the flames
That out beyond the range come billowing fast,
Though yet unseen from thence – till, with a hoarse
And pouncing swoop, as of a hurricane,
Furiously siezing on the drouth-sered brakes
That shag the terrace, all their serpent shapes
Rush upward, glaring into sudden view,
And ghastly prominence; – then quick as thought,
All culminating in the blast, they bend
Sheer o'er the oaks wherein the birds abide!
At once are these in flight! But from above,
As suddenly, a mightier burst of flame
Outsheeteth o'er them: down they dip – but it
Keeps swooping with them even to the ground,
(Drawn thither by dead leaf-drifts, layer on layer
There lodged, as rain-swept from the heights above)
And where, a moment after, all are seen
To writhe convulsed – blasted and plumeless all!

   Out through the Forest, looming through the smoke
Where dim and mist-like, farthest forth it rolls,
Behold how furiously a horseman rides,
Hitherward tending. 'Tis a Messenger,
Sent from the nearest Station, though thus late,
To warn our people of the mighty Fire
Ere haply it reach them; – telling them in time
How there, so lately, its red waves had brought
Sudden destruction and wide loss – and then
Surged on illimitably through the woods,
Bearing right hitherward. Bravely on he steers
To where the fronting flames from either hand
Are closing to a gap. No other way,
All round, is open; and he nears it – But

129

Too late, alas! or so to those it seems
Who watch him from the clear. Too late, for lo,
The lines of fire (ere't seemed they would) have met,
And man and horse are swallowed out of sight
In one red gloom of mingled flame and smoke!
But for a moment only. Bursting forth,
As if developed from that lurid mass,
The noble hackney brings his rider through
All but unsinged. Our friends hurrah; and he
Soon joins them – welcome, though too late for help.

   Thus through the day the conflagration raged:
And when the wings of night o'erspread the scene,
Not even *they*, with all their world-wide pomp
Of starry blazonries, wore such a live
And aggregated glory to the eye,
As did the blazing dead-wood of the Forest –
On all hands blazing! Yet, far off, the dells
Lay like black gouts amid the general view
Of glimmering heights, which through the red light showed
Like some imaginary waste of Hell,
Painted in blood.

           But nearer, all the view
Was frightfully brilliant! From vast hollow trunks
Whose ponderous heads, in some great hurricane,
Where the bole narrowed had been snapt away,
The wild fire, with a sudden roar, would burst
In quivering columns chapitered with smoke
Half turned itself into a lurid glow,
As out of craters; or some carious bough,
The white heat seething from its spouty flaws,
Would, with a dread crash, from the hill-top trees
(Massing aloft over the gleamy dark
That shut in under some o'erjutting steep)
Swoop flaming, like an unsphered group of stars,
Torn and disfeatured in their ruinous fall,
And run together, – a swift dropping mass
Of luminous points, and flaring limbs, that met
All in one fiery train, back-streaming, till
It shattered as it struck the blackened vale
Into a cloud of quick resulting sparks,
And igneous dust! Or down the flickery glades
Ghastfully glaring, huge dry-mouldered gums

Stood 'mid their living kin as barked throughout
With eating fire expelling arrowy jets
Of blue-lipt, intermitting, gaseous flame,
Boles, branches, – all! like vivid ghosts of trees,
Frightful to see! – the immemorial Wood's
First hoary Fathers wrapt in burning shrouds,
Come from the past, within the Whiteman's pale,
To typify their doom. Such was the prospect!
Illuminated cities were but jests
Compared with it for splendor. But enough!
Where are the words to paint the million shapes
And unimaginable freaks of Fire,
When holding thus its monster carnival
In the primeval Forest all night long?

Preface to The Kangaroo Hunt

The first draft of the following Descriptive Poem was written many years ago, and referred to a period yet earlier, when the habits and pastimes of the inland dwelling Colonists were much more simple than they are at present, and when the horse was a possession too rare and valuable to be used in the rough hap-hazzards of a Bush Hunt, or even, except on great emergency, upon a mountain journey. Nay, during the early Colonial period to which it refers, even a gun was a somewhat scarce article, or one not often employed in Kangaroo hunting, while powder and shot were far too expensive to be blazed away freely. That *golden* prosperity which has made us so luxurious, and even prodigal, as a community of Colonists, is of a comparatively recent growth – as recent in fact as the auriferous discoveries which it followed, and which have mainly contributed to it.

The Poem is designed to picture a morning in the mountains, with a Kangaroo Hunt for the centre and pivot of the performance: *one* hunt only, because there would be too much sameness in a succession of 'runs' for particular description. For the purpose, however, of bringing as many characteristic circumstances as possible into this *one*, the kangaroo is carried over more ground than he would, with swift hounds at his heels, be likely to cover in an actual case, unless endowed with an extraordinary degree of both speed and endurance. But to render this the more probable, he is allowed, through an error of his pursuers, to get considerably a-head of them about the middle of the Hunt. And also, in keeping the hunters well up with the hounds, for the sake of imparting a wholeness and an animation to that part of the description, many advantages are thrown into them, in the cast of the ground and otherwise, which they would not often be favored with in any given locality.

The personal digressions in the fifth Part are not indulged in for their own sake merely. They are a part of the design of the Poem, being introduced for the purpose of filling up as pleasingly as the scope and keeping of the subject admitted, the pause which is there given to the description of the kangaroo's flight and the pursuit of the hounds; – there happening to be, in these respects, just then, nothing worthy of particular mention, after the advantage accruing to the former, through an error of the latter, which is noticed in the conclusion of Part IV.

The Scenery of the Poem, as a whole, does not answer to any particular locality. But such of the more remarkable features of Australian scenery as the Author was acquainted with, have been brought together (as in a pictorial composition) in the several descriptions. Those, for example, in the body of the piece, are suitable, in the main, to those of almost any of our wild mountain districts; while the prospect given in the Introduction (as the whole of the first Part may be considered) might be made, with trifling allowances, to apply to many of the newer Settlements on the banks of our inland streams – around which the face of nature, under the improving operations of civilised man, has already yielded up much, and is daily resigning more, of its aboriginal cast and character. And on this head it is to be further observed, that the mountains amongst which the Hunt is supposed to be laid, though bold and even sublime in many of their aspects, are not generally either very lofty or very precipitous. They are, in fact, craggy hills rather than mountains – the real mountains ranging immediately at the back, though often extending forward into the midst of them, in the shape of a gigantic bluff or of an abrupt elbow: and though in many places perilously craggy, they are yet wound along and shelfed as if it were by grassy terraces, almost void of rocks, and letting off laterally into slopes of open forest – the whole together forming an accessible though a somewhat broken and difficult coursing country.

But in the above scenic conditions, there are ample scope and materials for the picturesque: and, moreover, I believe that, as an object of sublimity, there is no great difference between a mountain two thousand feet high and one twice that height, when beheld separately. Nay, the lesser mountain, if more precipitous, and bold in its outlines, will be even the sublimer object of the twain – and this, too, the nearer we approach it. Mere bulk, as an element of the wonderful, is more dependant upon the bodily eye, and also upon instant objective comparison, than any other consituent of the Sublime; and hence it is, that over a certain height in a mountain – say two thousand feet or so – it requires a very great addition indeed, to make a difference that is immediately or ocularly perceptible – except at such a distance *on the horizon*, as would all but nullify the effect of any sublime superiority therefrom accruing.

At all events, for poetic purposes, mere bulk need not to be very much relied upon or primarily sought after. The suggestiveness of the treatment in matters of magnitude – the imaginative manner of handling them – is nearly everything. Hence Olympus and the highest Himilayan, to which it is but a mole-hill, may be made to look equally mighty in verse. Nay, with the Ideal bending over it, and enskying it as it were with the poetic heaven of the historic Past, the larger majesties will dwell, like the Homeric Gods, upon the peaks of Olympus. The scenic imagery of the Bible, though often so ruggedly sublime, was the product of a country whose mountains, speaking literally, are but rocky hills. See also the mighty effect which Shakspare has wrought, in poetic picture, and by virtue of a certain mental intensity of treatment, out of the comparatively insignificant Cliff of Dover. Nay, a rock rift of but twenty feet in depth is a sturdy miniature of the wildest Alpine gorge, and when beheld with such a reference, through an imaginary process of self-diminution, becomes savagely sublime. So much does the grandeur of bulk depend upon the grandeur of form; and both these again, however strikingly blended, may be raised almost immeasurably by poetic intensification.

Moreover, – except when a limited local reference happens to be historical to the subject, – the Poet, in picturing nature, should never pin himself to the particular, or to the locally present. The Proseman may do this at all times, and insist upon the merit of his parochial closeness; but the Poet must not: for if he do, his draft will be but a vague *account* at the best, – not a poetic picture. But he should paint her primarily through his imagination; and thus the striking features and colors of many scenes, which lie permanently gathered in his memory, becoming, with their influences, idealised in the process, will be essentially transfused up *few*; or even upon *one* scene – one happy embodiment of her wildest freaks, or one Eden-piece embathed with a luminous atmosphere of sentiment. But never by wholesale will this transfusion be made, or indiscriminately; but in judicious keeping with the design and scope of his subject as a picture, and exactly according to its special limits and likelihoods as a landscape. And though what is thus painted may be raised in beauty or wildness above the average of any given exhibition of these qualities, it may yet, as a picture, be profoundly true to Nature, or to that flow and expression of character which such qualities best conform to, when we either locally exalt or locally concentrate her style. Thus it is truth sublimated, compressed, epitomised; – truth raised to its height, or strained away through the alembic of invention from whatever is unsightly or merely wearisome, and presented anew, though in vision, in its selectest forms and possibilities. For though, as a matter of art, it comes to *us* or is presented through the invention of the Poet, yet to *him* it came, – not literally, as in the picture before us, but in all the elements of that picture, – direct from Nature. In fine, if the Poet has been wholly true to his missionary insight in the first place, and to his re-creative instincts in the next, the license taken, and the modifications made by art, will reach only to its pictorial manner and assemblage of objects: in its spirit it will still be very Nature; while in its effect, as an aesthetic success, it will be Something yet more precious – a mind-enclosed possession, and thence a 'joy for ever'.

The versification of the Poem throughout is designedly irregular, or what is commonly thought to be so, – and indeed, *is* so, under the established standards. But when composing it, I concieved that such an unconfined, many-metred structure of verse as might be varied and paragraphically moulded (after the manner of a musical movement, to the peculiar demands of every occasion, and appear therefore to result spontaneously from the very nature of the things depicted, would be most conducive to the effective treatment of a subject, the art-interest of which would depend so largely upon its metrical vehicle. And though I have since become aware that Coleridge has said something of a like purport in reference to the versification of his Christabel, yet I can affirm that when writing this piece I had never read a line of that Poem; or indeed, of any production whatever that was professedly imitative of it, either in respect of its style, or in any other respect. My design, therefore, was so far original. And this design, I am sure, was in itself a good one, however I may have failed in carrying it out. But I do not think that I have therein failed. On the contrary, I flatter myself, that the style of the verse, though it may not at first be thought altogether pleasing by some readers, will yet, on a second and more studied perusal, commend itself to the critical, as being in the main appropriate to the matter – and if so, *essentially* harmonious.

Euroma, 1863

A Storm in the Mountains

Part I

A lonely Boy, for [far] venturing from his home,
Out on the half-wild herd's dim tracks I roam:
A lonely Truant, numbering years eleven,
'Mid rock-browed mountains heaping up to heaven!
Here huge-piled ledges, ribbing outward, stare
Down into haggard chasms; onward, there,
The vast backed ridges are all rent in jags,
Or hunched with cones, or pinnacled with crags.
A rude peculiar world, the prospect lies
Bounded in circuit by the bending skies.

• A STORM IN THE MOUNTAINS •

    Now at some stone tank scooped out by the shocks
Of rain-floods plunging from upper rocks,
Whose liquid disc, in its undimpled rest,
Glows like a mighty gem, brooching the mountain's breast,
I drink, and muse, – or mark the wide spread herd,
Or list the tinkling of the dingle-bird;
And now tow'rds some wild-hanging shade I stray,.
To shun the bright oppression of the day:
For round each crag, and o'er each bosky swell,
The fierce refracted heat flares visible –
Lambently restless, like the dazzling hem
Of some else-viewless veil held trembling over them.

    A change is felt – a change that yet reveals
A something only that mere instinct feels,
Why congregate the swallows in the air,
And northward then in rapid flight repair?
At once unsettled, and all roaming slow
With heads declined, why do the oxen low?
With sudden swelling din, remote, yet harsh,
Why roar the bull-frogs in the tea-tree marsh?
Why cease the locusts* to throng up in flight,
And clap their gay wings in the fervent light?
Why climb they, bodingly demure, instead,
The tallest spear-grass to the bending head?
Instinctively along the sultry sky,
I turn a listless, yet enquiring eye;
And mark that now, with a most gradual pace,
A solemn trance creams gradual o'er its face;
Slow, but inevitable – wide about
On all hands from the South effusing out:

* What in this country we call the *grasshopper* is no doubt the 'locust' of the Bible – the locust that John the Baptist made his dinner of in the wilderness. The Blacks often eat them as a food; and even the native dog not only affects them as a dainty, but seems to thrive upon them. In the right season, and in the places where they happen to be plentiful, he may sometimes be seen jumping after them as they fly up before him, for several hours at a stretch. On the other hand, what we Australians call *locusts* of all kinds, are but various species of the *cicada*. And while on this note, I may as well mention, that just before a storm, the locusts or grasshoppers inhabiting such flats and basins as are liable to be suddenly flooded by it, will all be seen instinctively mounting to the tassals of the reeds and higher grasses, – exactly as described in the text, – so as to be as high and dry as possible in the event of a local deluge. Verily, what we call *instinct*, is a thing altogether wonderful.

135

Yon clouds that late were laboring past the sun,
Reached by its sure arrest, one after one,
Come to a heavy halt; – as travellers see
In the wide wilderness of Araby,
Some pilgrim horde at even, band by band,
Halting amid the grey and ceaseless sand.
Thence down descending, its dull slumbrous weight
Sullenly settles on the mountain's great
Upheaving heads, until the airs that played
About their rugged temples – all are laid:
While drawing nearer far off heights appear,
As in a dream's wild prospect – strangely near!
Till into wood resolves their robe of blue,
And the grey crags come bluffly into view.
– Such are the signs and tokens that presage
A Summer Hurricane's forthcoming rage.

At length the South sends out her cloudy heaps,
And up the glens a dusky dimness creeps.
The birds, late warbling in the hanging green
Of steep-set brakes, seek now some safer screen, –
Skimming in silence o'er the ominous scene.
The herd in doubt no longer wanders wide,
But, fast ingathering, throngs yon mountain's side,
Whose echoes, surging to its tramp, might seem
The muttered troubles of some Titan's dream.

Fast the dim legions of the mustering Storm
Throng denser, or protruding columns form;
While splashing forward from their cloudy lair,
Convolving flames, like scouting dragons, glare:
Low thunders follow, laboring up the sky;
And as forerunning blasts go blaring by,
At once the Forest, with a mighty stir,
Bows, as in homage to the Thunderer!

Hark! from the dingoes' blood-polluted dens,
In the gloom-hidden chasms of the glens,
Long fitful howls wail up; and in the blast
Strange hissing whispers seem to huddle past;
As if the dread stir had aroused from sleep
Weird Spirits, cloistered in yon cavy steep,

(On which, in the grim Past, some Cain's offence
Hath haply outraged Heaven!) – and who, from thence
Wrapt in the boding vapours, rose amain
To wanton in the wild-willed Hurricane!

   The glow of day is quenched – expunged the sun
By cloud on cloud dark-rolling into one
Tremendous mass of latent thunder – spread
Wide out, and over every mountain's head,
Whose sable bosom, as the storm-blast sweeps
Its surface, heaves into enormous heaps,
And seems a pendent ocean to the view,
With weltering whale-like forms all hugely roughend through.

Part II

   Yet see in the Storm's front, as void of dread,
How sails yon Eagle like a black flag spread
Before it – coming! On his wide wings weighed,
Hardly he seems to move, from hence surveyed;
When, far aloft, a bulging mass of gloom
That bends out o'er him, bloating as with doom,
Grows frightfully luminous! Short stops his flight!
His dark form shrivels in the blasting light!
And then as follows a sharp thunderous sound,
Falls whizzing, stone-like, lifeless to the ground!

Now like a shudder at great Nature's heart
The turmoil grows. Now Wonder, with a start,
Marks where, right overhead, wild Thor careers,
Girt with black Horrors and wide-flaming Fears!
Arriving thunders, mustering on his path,
Swell more and more the roarings of his wrath,
As out in widening circles they extend –
And then – at once – in utter silence end.

   Portentous silence! Time keeps breathing past –
Yet it continues! May this marvel last?
This wild weird silence in the midst of gloom
So manifestly big with latent doom?
Tingles the boding ear; and up the glens
Instinctive dread comes howling from the wild-dogs' dens.

Terrific Vision! Heaven's great cieling splits,
And a vast globe of writhing fire emits,
Which, flanking out in one continuous stream,
Spans the black concave like a burning beam,
A moment; – then, from end to end, it shakes
With a quick motion – and in thunder breaks!
Peal rolled on peal! while heralding the sound,
As each concussion thrills the solid ground,
Fierce glares coil snake-like round the rocky wens
Of the *red* hills, or hiss into the glens;
Or thick through heaven like flaming falchions swarm,
Cleaving the teeming cisterns of the Storm,
From which rain-torrents, (searching every gash)
Split by the blast, come sheeting, with a dash
Most multitudinous – down through the trees,
And 'gainst the smoking crags that beetle over these!

On yon grey Peak, with rock-encrusted roots,
The seeming Patriarch of the Wood upshoots,
In whose proud-spreading top's imperial height,
The mountain Eagle loveth most to 'light:
Now dimly seen through the tempestuous air,
His form seems harrowed by a mad despair,
As with his ponderous arms uplifted high,
He wrestles with the Storm and threshes at the sky!
But not for long. Up in the lurid air,
A swift red bolt is heard to hurtle there –
A dread crash follows – and the Peak is bare!
Huge fragments, hurrying from its shattered cone,
Wide in the murky air are seen alone –
Huge shapeless fragments round about it cast,
Like crude-wing'd, mad-limbed Monsters squandering in the blast!

The duskness thickens! With despairing cry
From shattering boughs the rain-drenched parrots fly!
Loose rocks wash rumbling from the mountains round,
And half the forest strews the smoking ground!
Stemm'd by the wet crags the blasts wilder moan,
And the caves labor with a ghostlier groan!
Resistless torrents down the gorges flow
With knasshing clamours harshening as they go;
And where from craggy bluffs their volumes leap,
Bear with them – down, in many a whirling heap,
Those sylvan wrecks that littered late the path
Of the loud Hurricane's all-trampling wrath;

While to their dread percussions inward sent,
The hearts of the great hills beat with astonishment!

   Strange darings seize me, witnessing this strife
Of Nature; while, as heedless of my life,
I stand exposed. And does some destined charm
Hold me secure from elemental harm,
That in the mighty riot I may find
How through all being works the light of Mind?
Yea, through the strikingly external see
My novel Soul's divulging energy!
Spirit transmuting into forms of thought
What but for its cognition were *as nought*!
Soul wildly drawn abroad – a Pròtean force
Clothing with higher life the Tempest in its course.

            * * *

The Storm is past. Yet booming on afar
Is heard the rattling of Thor's thunder-car,
And that low muffled moaning, as of grief,
Which follows, with a wood-sigh wide and brief.
The clouds break up. The sun's forth bursting rays
Clothe the wet landscape with a spangling blaze.
The birds begin to sing a lively strain,
And merry echoes ring it o'er again.
The clustered herd is spreading out to graze,
Though lessening torrents still a hundred ways
Flash downward, and from many a tanky ledge
A mantling gush comes quick and shining o'er the edge.

            * * *

'Tis evening; and the torrents' furious flow
Hath now subsided in the laks [lakes] below.
O'er all the freshened scene no sound is heard,
Save the short twitter of some busied bird,
Or a faint rustle caused amongst the trees
By wasting fragments of a broken breeze.
Round with a heightened buoyancy I stroll,
And a new happiness o'erflows my soul,
As from some cause beyond the reach of thought,
And which this notion has within me wrought
Through instinct only, that the Storm to day,
Hath haply purged some pestilence away,
Whose sultry venom in all nature's ways
Would else have lurked for many doomful days:

And hence, even 'mid the sylvan carnage spread
O'er every turn in the wild paths I tread,
Full many a flowery nook and sunny brow
Presents some pleasantness unmarked till now.

   Thus, when the elements of social life
Burst with a soul-quake into mortal strife,
Some prophet feeling, we know not from whence,
Doth moralise the agony; and thence
Wished Peace, returning, like a bird of calm,
Brings to the wounded world a doubly-valued balm.

The Creek of the Four Graves

Part I

I verse a Settler's tale of olden times –
One told me by our sage friend, Egremont;
Who then went forth, meetly equipt, with four
Of his most trusty and adventurous men
Into the wilderness, – went forth to seek
New streams and wider pastures for his fast
Augmenting flocks and herds. On foot were all,
For horses then were beasts of too great price
To be much ventured upon mountain routes,
And over wild wolds clouded up with brush,
And cut with marshes, perilously deep.

   So went they forth at dawn: and now the sun
That rose behind them as they journeyed out,
Was firing with his nether rim a range
Of unknown mountains that, like ramparts, towered
Full in their front, and his last glances fell
Into the gloomy forest's eastern glades
In golden masses, transiently, or flashed
Down on the windings of a nameless Creek,
That noiseless ran betwixt the pioneers
And those new Apennines; – ran, shaded up
With boughs of the wild willow, hanging mixed
From either bank, or duskily befringed

With upward tapering, feathery swamp-oaks –
The sylvan eyelash always of remote
Australian waters, whether gleaming still
In lake or pool, or bickering along
Between the marges of some eager stream.

   Before then, thus extended, wilder grew
The scene each moment – and more beautiful!
For when the sun was all but sunk below
Those barrier mountains, – in the breeze that o'er
Their rough enormous backs deep fleeced with wood
Came whispering down, the wide upslanting sea
Of fanning leaves in the descending rays
Danced interdazzingly, as if the trees
That bore them, were all thrilling, – tingling all
Even to the roots for very happiness:
So prompted from within, so sentient, seemed
The bright quick motion – wildly beautiful.

   But when the sun had wholly disappeared
Behind those mountains – O what words, what hues
Might paint the wild magnificence of view
That opened westward! Out extending, lo,
The heights rose crowding, with their summits all
Dissolving, as it seemed, and partly lost
In the exceeding radiancy aloft;
And thus transfigured, for awhile they stood
Like a great company of Archeons, crowned
With burning diadems, and tented o'er
With canopies of purple and of gold!

   Here halting wearied, now the sun was set,
Our travellers kindled for their first night's camp
The brisk and crackling fire, which also looked
A wilder creature than 'twas elsewhere wont,
Because of the surrounding savageness.
And soon in cannikins the tea was made,
Fragrant and strong; long fresh-sliced rashers then
Impaled on whittled skewers, were deftly broiled
On the live embers, and when done, tranferred
To quadrants from an ample damper cut,
Their only trenchers, – soon to be dispatched
With all the savoury morsels they sustained,
By the keen tooth of healthful appitite.

And as they supped, birds of new shape and plume,
And wild strange voice, nestward repairing by,
Oft took their wonder; or betwixt the gaps
In the ascending forest growths they saw
Perched on the bare abutments of the hills,
Where haply yet some lingering gleam fell through,
The wallaroo* look forth: till eastward all
The view had wasted into formless gloom,
Night's front; and westward, the high massing woods
Steeped in a swart but mellowed Indian hue –
A deep dusk loveliness, – lay ridged and heaped
Only the more distinctly for their shade
Against the twilight heaven – a cloudless depth
Yet luminous with sunset's fading glow;
And thus awhile, in the lit dusk, they seemed
To hang like mighty pictures of themselves
In the still chambers of some vaster world.

The silent business of their supper done,
The Echoes of the solitary place,
Came as in sylvan wonder wide about
To hear, and imitate tentatively,
Strange voices moulding a strange speech, as then
Within the pleasant purlieus of the fire
Lifted in glee – but to be hushed erelong,
As with the night in kindred darkness came
O'er the adventurers, each and all, some sense –
Some vague-felt intimation from without,
Of danger, lurking in its forest lairs.

But nerved by habit, and all settled soon
About the well-built fire, whose nimble tongues
Sent up continually a strenuous roar
Of fierce delight, and from their fuming pipes
Full charged and fragrant with the Indian weed,
Drawing rude comfort, – typed without, as 'twere,
By tiny clouds over their several heads
Quietly curling upward; – thus disposed
Within the pleasant firelight, grave discourse
Of their peculiar business brought to each
A steadier mood, that reached into the night.

* A kind of large Kangaroo peculiar to the higher and more difficult mountains.

The simple subject to their minds at length
Fully discussed, their couches they prepared
Of rushes, and the long green tresses pulled
Down from the boughs of the wild willows near.
Then four, as pre-arranged, stretched out their limbs
Under the dark arms of the forest trees
That mixed aloft, high in the starry air,
In arcs and leafy domes whose crossing curves
And roof-like features, – blurring as they ran
Into some denser intergrowth of sprays, –
Were seen in mass traced out against the clear
Wide gaze of heaven; and trustful of the watch
Kept near them by their thoughtful Master, soon
Drowsing away, forgetful of their toil,
And of the perilous vast wilderness
That lay around them like a spectral world,
Slept, breathing deep; – whilst all things there as well
Showed slumbrous, – yea, the circling forest trees,
Their foremost boles carved from a crowded mass
Less visible, by the watchfire's bladed gleams,
As quick and spicular, from the broad red ring
Of its more constant light they ran in spurts
Far out and under the umbrageous dark;
And even the shaded and enormous mounts,
Their bluff brows glooming through the stirless air,
Looked in their quiet solemnly asleep:
Yea, thence surveyed, the Universe might have seemed
Coiled in vast rest, – only that one dim cloud,
Diffused and shapen liked a huge spider,
Crept as with scrawling legs along the sky;
And that the stars, in their bright orders, still
Cluster by cluster, glowingly revealed
As this slow cloud moved on, – high over all, –
Looked wakeful – yea, looked thoughtful in their peace.

Part II

Meanwhile the cloudless eastern heaven had grown
More and more luminous – and now the Moon
Up from behind a giant hill was seen
Conglobing, till – a mighty mass – she brought
Her under border level with its cone,
As thereon it were resting: when, behold
A wonder! Instantly that cone's whole bulk
Erewhile so dark, seemed inwardly a-glow
With her instilled irradiance; while the trees
That fringed its outline, – their huge statures dwarfed
By distance into brambles, and yet all
Clearly defined against her ample orb, –
Out of its very disc appeared to swell
In shadowy relief, as they had been
All sculptured from its substance as she rose.

   Thus o'er that dark height her great orb arose,
Till her full light, in silvery sequence still
Cascading forth from ridgy slope to slope,
Like the dropt foldings of a lucent veil,
Chased mass by mass the broken darkness down
Into the dense-brushed valleys, where it crouched,
And shrank, and struggled, like a dragon doubt
Glooming some lonely spirit that doth still
Resist the Truth with obstinate shifts and shows,
Though shining out of heaven, and from defect
Winning a triumph that might else not be.

   There standing in his lone watch, Egremont
On all this solemn beauty of the world,
Looked out, yet wakeful; for sweet thoughts of home
And all the sacred charities it held,
Ingathered to his heart, as by some nice
And subtle interfusion that connects
The loved and cherished (then the most, perhaps,
When absent, or when passed, or even when *lost*)
With all serene and beautiful and bright
And lasting things of Nature. So then thought
The musing Egremont: when sudden – hark!
A bough crackt loudly in a neighboring brake,
And drew at once, as with alarum, all
His spirits thitherward in wild surmise.

But summoning caution, and back stepping close
Against the shade-side of a bending gum,
With a strange horror gathering to his heart,
As if his blood were charged with insect life
And writhed along in clots, he stilled himself,
Listening long and heedfully, with head
Bent forward sideways, till his held breath grew
A pang, and his ears rung. But Silence there
Had recomposed her ruffled wings, and now
Brooded it seemed even stillier than before,
Deep nested in the darkness: so that he
Unmasking from the cold shade, grew erelong
More reassured from wishing to be so,
And to muse Memory's suspended mood,
Though with an effort, quietly recurred.

But there again – crack upon crack! And hark!
O Heaven! have Hell's worst fiends burst howling up
Into the death-doom'd world? Or whence, if not
From diabolic range, could surge a yell
So horrible as that which now affrights
The shuddering dark! Beings as fell are near!
Yea, Beings, in their dread inherited hate
And deadly enmity, as vengeful, come
In vengeance! For behold, from the long grass
And nearer brakes, a semi-belt of stript
And painted Savages divulge at once
Their bounding forms! – full in the flaring light
Thrown outward by the fire, that roused and lapped
The rounding darkness with its ruddy tongues
More fiercely than before, – as though even *it*
Had felt the sudden shock the air received
From those dire cries, so terrible to hear!

A moment in wild agitation seen
Thus, as they bounded up, on then they came
Closing, with weapons brandished high, and so
Rushed in upon the sleepers! three of whom
But started, and then weltered prone beneath
The first fell blow dealt down on each by three
Of the most stalwart of their pitiless foes!
But One again, and yet again, heaved up –
Up to his knees, under the crushing strokes
Of huge-clubbed nulla-nullas, till his own

Warm blood was blinding him! For he was one
Who had with Misery nearly all his days
Lived lonely, and who therefore, in his soul,
Did hunger after hope, and thirst for what
Hope still had promised him, – some taste at least
Of human good however long deferred,
And now he could not, even in dying, loose
His hold on life's poor chances of tomorrow –
Could not but so dispute the terrible fact
Of death, even in Death's presence! Strange it is:
Yet oft 'tis seen that Fortune's pampered child
Consents to his untimely power with less
Reluctance, less despair, than does the wretch
Who hath been ever blown about the world
The straw-like sport of Fate's most bitter blasts,
Vagrant and tieless; – ever still in him
The craving spirit thus grieves to itself:

   'I never yet was happy – never yet
Tasted unmixed enjoyment, and I would
Yet pass on the bright Earth that I have loved
Some season, though most brief, of happiness;
So should I walk thenceforward to my grave,
Wherever in her green maternal breast
It might await me, more than now prepared
To house me in its gloom, – resigned at heart,
Subjected to its certainty and soothed
Even by the consciousness of having shaped
Some personal good in being; – strong myself,
And strengthening others. But to have lived long years
Of wasted breath, because of woe and want,
And disappointed hope, – and now, at last,
To die thus desolate, is horrible!'

   And feeling thus through many foregone moods
Whose lines had in the temper of his soul
All mixed, and formed *one* habit, – that poor man,
Though the black shadows of untimely death,
Inevitably, under every stroke,
But thickened more and more, – against them still
Upstruggled, nor would cease: until one last
Tremendous blow, dealt down upon his head
As if in mercy, gave him to the dust
With all his many woes and frustrate hope.

Struck through with a cold horror, Egremont,
Standing apart, – yea, standing as it were
In marble effigy, saw this, saw all!
And when outthawing from his frozen heart
His blood again rushed tingling – with a leap
Awaking from the ghastly trance which there
Had bound him, as with chill petrific bonds,
He raised from instinct more than conscious thought
His death-charged tube, and at that murderous crew
Firing! saw one fall ox-like to the earth; –
Then turned and fled. Fast fled he, but as fast
His deadly foes went thronging on his track!
Fast! for in full pursuit, behind him yelled
Wild men whose wild speech hath no word for *mercy*!
And as he fled, the forest beasts as well,
In general terror, through the brakes a-head
Crashed scattering, or with maddening speed athwart
His course came frequent. On – still on he flies –
Flies for dear life! and still behind him hears
Nearer and nearer, the so rapid dig
Of many feet, – nearer and nearer still.

Part III

So went the chase! And now what should he do?
Abruptly turning, the wild Creek lay right
Before him! But no time was there for thought:
So on he kept, and from a bulging rock
That beaked the bank like a bare promontory,
Plunging right forth and shooting feet-first down,
Sunk to his middle in the flashing stream –
In which the imaged stars seemed all at once
To burst like rockets into one wild blaze
Of interwrithing light. Then wading through
The ruffled waters, forth he sprang and siezed
A snake-like root that from the opponent bank
Protruded, and round which his earnest fear
Did clench his cold hand like a clamp of steel,
A moment, – till as swiftly thence he swung
His dripping form aloft, and up the dark
O'erjutting ledge went clambering in the blind
And breathless haste of one who flies for life:
When its face – O verily our God
Hath those in his peculiar care for whom

The daily prayers of spotless Womanhood
And helpless Infancy, are offered up! –
When in its face a cavity he felt,
The upper earth of which in one rude mass
Was held fast bound by the enwoven roots
Of two old trees, – and which, beneath the mould,
Just o'er the clammy vacancy below,
Twisted and lapped like knotted snakes, and made
A natural loft-work. Under this he crept,
Just as the dark forms of his hunters thronged
The bulging rock whence he before had plunged.

   Duskily visible, thereon a space
They paused to mark what bent his course might take
Over the farther bank, thereby intent
To hold upon the chase, which way soe'er
It might incline, more surely. But no form
Amongst the moveless fringe of fern was seen
To shoot up from its outline, – up and forth
Into the moonlight that lay bright beyond
In torn and shapeless blocks, amid the boles
And mixing shadows of the taller trees,
All standing now in the keen radiance there
So ghostly still, as in a solemn trance.
But nothing in the silent prospect stirred –
No fugitive apparition in the view
Rose, as they stared in fierce expectancy:
Wherefore they augured that their prey was yet
Somewhere between, – and the whole group with that
Plunged forward, till the fretted current boiled
Amongst their crowding trunks from bank to bank;
And searching thus the stream across, and then
Lengthwise, along the ledges, – combing down
Still, as they went, with dripping fingers, cold
And cruel as inquisitive, each clump
Of long flagged swamp-grass where it flourished high, –
The whole dark line passed slowly, man by man,
Athwart the cavity – so fearfully near,
That as they waded by the Fugitive
Felt the strong odor of their wetted skins
Pass with them, trailing as their bodies moved
Stealthily on, – coming with each, and going.

But their keen search was keen in vain. And now
Those wild men marvelled, – till, in consultation,
There grouped in dark knots standing in the stream
That glimmered past them, moaning as it went,
His vanishment, so passing strange it seemed,
They coupled with the mystery of some crude
Old fable of their race; and fear-struck all,
And silent, then withdrew. And when the sound
Of their receeding steps had from his ear
Died off, as back to the stormed Camp again
They hurried to despoil the yet warm dead,
Our Friend slid forth, and springing up the bank,
Renewed his flight, nor rested from it, till
He gained the welcoming shelter of his Home.

Return we for a moment to the scene
Of recent death. There the late flaring fire
Now smouldered, for its brands were strewn about,
And four stark corses plundered to the skin
And brutally mutilated, seemed to stare
With frozen eyeballs up into the pale
Round visage of the Moon, who, high in heaven,
With all her stars, in golden bevies, gazed
As peacefully down as on a bridal there
Of the warm Living – not, alas! on them
Who kept in ghastly silence through the night
Untimely spousals with a desert death.

O God! and thus this lovely world hath been
Accursed for ever by the bloody deeds
Of its prime Creature – Man. Erring or wise,
Savage or civilised, still hath he made
This glorious residence, the Earth, a Hell
Of wrong and robbery and untimely death!
Some dread Intelligence opposed to Good
Did, of a surety, over all the earth
Spread out from Eden – or it were not so!
For see the bright beholding Moon, and all
The radiant Host of Heaven, evince no touch
Of sympathy with Man's wild violence; –
Only evince in their calm course, their part
In that original unity of Love,
Which, like the soul that dwelleth in a harp,
Under God's hand, in the beginning, chimed

The sabbath concord of the Universe;
And look on a gay clique of maidens, met
In village tryst, and interwhirling all
In glad Arcadian dances on the green –
Or on a hermit, in his vigils long,
Seen kneeling at the doorway of his cell –
Or on a monster battle-field where lie
In sweltering heaps, the dead and dying both,
On the cold gory ground, – as they that night
Looked in bright peace, down on the doomful wild.

Afterwards there, for many changeful years,
Within a glade that sloped into the bank
Of that wild mountain Creek – midway within,
In partial record of a terrible hour
Of human agony and loss extreme,
Four grassy mounds stretched lengthwise side by side,
Startled the wanderer; – four long grassy mounds
Bestrewn with leaves, and withered spraylets, stript
By the loud wintry wingèd gales that roamed
Those solitudes, from the old trees which there
Moaned the same leafy dirges that had caught
The heed of dying Ages: these were all;
And thence the place was long by travellers called
The Creek of the Four Graves. Such was the Tale
Egremont told us of the wild old times.

Poetic Descriptions of Violent Death

Many [?] descriptions of violent death are met with [in] English poets, from Chaucer downwards: a [?] fact that might furnish matter for much characteristic speculation But it is not my present intention to travel beyond the fact itself, and the poetic effects of it.

* * *

In the description of Greysteel's death in the old heroic ballad there is a searching imaginative hardihood in the details which gives to the picture a terrible force of reality. It is at once dreadful and pathetic.

But I know of nothing so terrible in this kind, as Milton's account in Paradise Lost of the death of Abel. There is a destructive selectness in every word of it.

————————————— an altar as the landmark stood [?]
Rustic, of grassy sord: thither anon
A sweaty reaper from this tillage brought
First fruits, the green ear and the yellow sheaf,
Unculled, as came to hand; a shepherd next,
More meek, came with the firstlings of his flock
Choicest and best; then, sacrificing, laid
The inwards and their fat, with incense strowed,
On the cleft wood, and all due rites performed.
His offering soon propitious fire from heaven
Consumed with nimble glance, and grateful steam;
The other's not, for his was not sincere;
Whereat he inly raged, and, as they talked,
Smote him into the midriff with a stone
That beat out life; he fell; and, deadly pale,
Groaned out his soul with gushing blood effused.

Eden Lost

The only faithless thing is Man,
Whose evil plan
Excludes Man's brotherhood:
All else are trusty to the rod
And sireship of Almighty God,
But Man, in his lordly mood.

The honest moon pays down her light
In silver bright,
The sun in burning gold;
The stars above the hills that rise
Like thought informed and earnest eyes,
Keep compact as of old.

The birds their pristine glees prolong;
The flowery throng
Bloom as they bloomed alway;
The beasts amid the fields that won
Are loyal to their mould as on
Creation's earliest day.

'Tis Man alone – dishonest Man,
Who schemes a plan
Excluding brotherhood.
He only, with disnatured mind,
Becomes the Tyrant of his kind:
He! in his lordly mood.

But shall there not be yet a time
When this stern rhyme
Shall be no longer true?
When Love shall recreate the good
That guileless kept the brotherhood,
Man erst in Eden knew?

There shall! The very dream that we
Might faithful be,
Assures us that there *shall*!
When Freedom, to her mission true,
Shall commonise the lordly Few
By elevating All!

·5· Correspondence

Charles Harpur to Henry Parkes

Jerry's Plains
21st March, 1844

My dear Sir,
I hasten to acknowledge your kind present of Mrs Shelley's edition of her illustrious husband's poems, which has only just come to hand. The letter accompanying the books, for which I am also sincerely thankful, is dated, I perceive, as far back as Nov in last year. The delay in the conveyance which has evidently taken place, makes me very anxious lest you should attribute my silence since to any other than the true cause – my not being aware of your having again manifested in so flattering and substantial a manner your disinterested regard for a brother poet whom you have never seen, – and merely because you believe him to be a true child of Song. I say *substantial* above with reference to the beauty and rareness of your present, – but assure you, at the same time, that even a pin from you, given in token of good will, would be as gratefully received – aye, and as highly prized, in as far as tho' the commercial value of articles constitute a consideration. In nothing do I feel more honored and assured of my merit as a poet, than in the respect and attention with which you have from time to time gladdened my solitude. Accept then in return, all that I have at present to offer, the grateful friendship of a heart, which, though something less warm and trusting perhaps than it has been, is yet, I believe, true in its affections, and unspotted by the selfishness of the world.

As far back as in Jany. last, with a view of re-filling the 'cup of kindness' that had passed between us, I composed the following Sonnet to you, intending to publish it in the 'Register'; and I delayed to do so only, because my pieces latterly have been so fearfully misprinted therein, that I have felt quite savage while glancing them over – and I would not for a good deal that this Sonnet to you should meet a similar fate. However lamely expressed, I know you will give me credit for sincerity in the feeling it unfolds –

Sonnet to Henry Parkes

Dear Henry, tho' thy face I ne'er have seen,
  Nor heard thy voice – albeit that beams, I know,
  With goodness, and that this at times can flow
Melodious as a mountain stream – between
The waters of Port Jackson, and the scene
  Where now I muse, of rich, poor, high or low,
  There dwells not one that I so far would go
To talk with through the evening hours serene.
And when we yet shall meet, say, shall not we
  Be as old friends at once? and sit, and pour
Our souls together? which, so mixt, shall be
A brimming draught of thought-thick poesie –
  Even such as young Keats reel'd with, gazing o'er
The wondrous realms of Homer's minstrelsy.

You will see by the above, that I was not willing that the kindly feelings which had sprung up between us, should pass away with the blossoms of the Spring. No; I trust that they will ever continue to strengthen – and whenever my regards are turned Sydney-ward, I love to promise myself that they shall furnish the fruit of many an intellectual feast throughout the summer, and even the winter of our mortal days.

  I am exceedingly gratified by the selection you have made in your present. Shelley is a great favorite of mine; and besides I never saw the whole of his poems before. I had heard that Mrs Shelley was giving or had given to the world a completed edition of her husband's works, and longed particularly to see it – guess then the pleasure I was master of, or rather was mastered by, on recieving this same work in testimony of a friendship I value so much – and which evinces to me the fact, that disinterested literary kindness departed not the world with that most benevolent. – I love Shelley intensely; and yet I am not blind to his faults. If we would attain to highest excellence we must exercise the judgment with a rigid and resolute will, maugre our feelings to the contrary. Shelley has great faults, or rather great wants. His poems, though brilliant and beautiful as the splendors of sunset, are, I fear me, as unsubstantial as those fleeting hues. Not that I complain of their extreme visionariness; but that there is not enough of solid humanity wrought up with it to add strength and flavor. Even in the 'Revolt of Islam' the human interest is damaged by the airy-nothingness of the characters, and the impossibility of many of the incidents. Modern Ideality and Wonder, however wandering and willing, are yet, when over tasked, very apt to grow skittish, and to fly off at a tangent, with an appeal to Reason. Still Shelley is perhaps *my* greatest favorite; and though I may seem just now to be much 'critic-bitten', I have been throwing out such objections as I *apprehend*, rather than such as I *feel*. As a proof of this, it is scarcely an hour since I was gloating over the pages of your fine present with inexpressible satisfaction.

The generous object of your letter is, I take it, to incite me to renewed efforts. I also found a pen in the packet, which I understand to mean *write away*. I will obey in as far as I can; but I have to care so much for the mere crusts of life, that I am not often now in right tune for song. Your letter has, however, somewhat revived the 'bard in my bosom'. Whether any thing worth recording will be the result I cannot pretend just now to say. But we shall see. – I sometimes feel it hard to have written so much as I have already written with the power of publishing so little. Those sustained efforts upon which I would peril my poetic claims with considerable confidence I have not been able to give to the light at all. But perhaps all is for the best.

I hope you have not abandoned the Muse. I promise myself a treat, when I shall some day *forgather* with you, in pouring over the MSS of your late and more sustained pieces. Let me not be disappointed. You have the power if you have the will.

In conclusion, accept again my pledge of friendship, and allow me to solicit yours. Let us determine from this day, to be resolute so as to overcome whatever may tend to chill or diminish the brotherly feelings and kind wishes that have grown up so singularly between us. This is my firm resolve, and I assure myself that it will be yours – and

I subscribe myself therefore
Your friend and brother,
Charles Harpur

Excuse haste!

Charles Harpur to Nicol D. Stenhouse

Jerry's Plains
2 July, 1859

My dear Sir,
I have received your letter dated in May last more than a month after its date. The delay in its coming to hand, however, is partly (but not wholly) owing to my only using to send to the Post, which is 12 miles distant, about once a fortnight or so.

With regard to my giving a lecture at the Sydney School of Arts – say on Poetry, I cannot make any positive promise at present. It is quite likely, however, that I shall be able to do so. I am on the point of coming to some arrangements in my affairs here, that will unfasten my social chain for a time, and if I can then come to Sydney for the purpose of giving the said lecture, I will. I will in the meantime prepare it, and then, before the season is over, it is quite likely that, with it in my pocket, I shall be able to pay a flying visit to Sydney. When the coast is clear for my doing so, I will write and let you know, but I cannot yet make any more positive promise than this.

My life here is an extremely wearisome one. For example, every day, from light to dark, hitherto through the whole of this winter, I have been occupied in matters of pure labor. I carry a book about with me, in my pocket, for a fortnight at a stretch, without being able to snatch time enough to glance over even so much as a page of it: and this frets me more perhaps than anything besides. You, my dear Sir, can have no idea of the care required and the labor imposed by sheep, on an indifferent run in a bad season. Off the spot, the bare truth in this respect is well nigh incredible. But I am now about letting mine out on terms, with the view of turning my attention to something else. I have not a sufficient number to be able to work them smoothly, and I can no longer consent to be thus utterly swamped in the care of those I have. Set on terms, they will secure me a slight income, and so far assist me in trying some other line of life.

You assure me you wish to see me, and certainly I myself shall be drawn Sydney-ward, not so much by any audiance possible to the School of Arts, as by my desire to see you, and a few other persons, who are I think related to me in mind – that is, spiritually. But no doubt *you* will be disappointed in *me*. I have so long lived solitary, or amongst those with whom I have so few values and feelings in common, that conversation has become somewhat difficult to me from sheer disuse. When our best words all fly over the heads of our companions, we come to give up talking. But the social ice thus induced may break in your presence – nay, I even fore-feel that in some measure it will.

         I am, my dear Sir,
         very faithfully yours,
         Chas: Harpur

(Thereafter follows a poem on Coleridge's 'Christabel' entitled 'A Poem on a Poem'. (Ed.))

Charles Harpur to Nicol D. Stenhouse

                    Araluen,
                    12 November, 1859

My dear Sir,
I have nothing to write about – positively nothing. This is about as dreary a place as could well be imagined. There is nothing but grim mountains and as grim diggers all around me. In the mountains there is some distinctive character which I may yet turn to account – but in the diggers aforesaid, none – only a sort of gold-madness, varied at short intervals by a very decided rum-madness. So you see I have nothing just now worth writing about; and only take up my pen for the purpose of transcribing a poem for you – just to show that I am thinking about you, being indeed,
                    Yours ever devotedly,
                    Charles Harpur.

(Thereafter follows the poem 'Humanity', see p.28, initialled by Harpur. (Ed.))

Henry Kendall to Charles Harpur

                    Kingston. Newtown
                    Sep 25. 1862

Dear Mr Harpur,
Your welcome letter came to hand on Tuesday, and I hasten at this – my earliest opportunity, to reply to it. I must acknowledge that I was disappointed at not receiving any answer to my last; thinking the silence had proceeded from some fault in the construction of my boyish epistle. But your kind explanation relieved me greatly, and I can well imagine how your time is taken up where you are.

    I am very anxious to correspond with you: being assured that, mentally, I shall gain much by your letters. For we cannot leave a cedar grove without carrying away some of the fragrance, and the words of Genius may be fitly associated with the perfume-scattering leaves of those beautiful trees. I feel already deeply indebted to you for the great good and large comfort I have derived from your writings. There is no living author to whom I could turn and say as much. This may be a necessary result of my Australian birth and education. But, strangely fascinated by almost everything you have published, I have always looked upon you as the man who alone could express what I had so often dimly thought. While looking round upon external Nature, *some* of us see and feel *that* which we afterwards lose sight of and forget, until we find it, photographed as it were, in the luminous 'limning' of the true poet. I think that there is a fearful gap between thought and language. Perhaps there is no rarer endowment of the poet than the gift of exact expression – the power of subjugating language to thought; so he can conscientiously feel that the whole truth which was in him has been laid before the World in all its unclouded simplicity. How often, burning with the secret power within, do men feel they are incapable of manifesting themselves except through the medium of a dim – a cloudy ambiguity of words, which either distort the idea they yearn to convey, or else give but its bloodless and inanimate outline! I feel there is little discrepancy between conception and execution in your poems, and am satisfied your Ideal, with all its delicate lights and shadows, could not, *in any other dress*, be presented to us in its entire integrity. I speak for myself, and I trust, for thousands of my countrymen who have yet to read, to learn, and to enjoy.

Very likely I have not read half that which you have published; indeed only by looking over the files of the old 'Empire', and the 'Australian Home Companion', have I become acquainted with any of it. The 'People's Advocate' was before my time, and no copies are now obtainable. In the beginning of the present year, however, I secured a copy of the volume containing the 'Bushrangers', and a noble poem headed 'The Creek of the Four Graves'. I *know* that a counterpart of 'Egremont' has been with me in a like grand evening Forest, where the fire looked 'a wilder creature' than it would have seemed elsewhere, 'because of the surrounding savageness'; and where we for a moment appeared to be part of a colossal picture 'hung in some vaster World'. And I am *sure* we have watched the same solitary star which moved 'so thoughtfully awake' over that vast Australian gloom. One of your old calumniators was frightened back to his native mud, after hearing me read the 'Creek of the Four Graves'. The 'Tower of the Dream' is another of my favorites. One of the similies in that poem is the finest I have met with *anywhere*; and the song of the Spirit is so wildly – so strangely beautiful that one *might* imagine it to be conceived, as 'Kubla Khan' was, in a Dream. I don't care much for 'Yes' – one of Mr Stenhouse's pets – but 'Mary', 'In Yon Green Wood', and 'Cora' are indeed lovely. This, from 'Cora', haunts me whenever I turn to the sunset:

> 'Bright garments of a Spirit bright,
> That even in the shroud
> Were *like the sunset's golden light*
> Within *a lifeless cloud!*'

'Finish of Style' has all the 'bloom of unhandled grapes' about it, and the second of your 'Poems of Melancholy' sounds the very depths of feeling. I do not care much for what has been printed of 'Genius Lost', although there are so *many* fine passages in it. Perhaps it proceeds from my having no great sympathy for Chatterton. You must forgive me for being so candid. The extracts from 'King Saul' have truly a rich, Oriental flush around them, and are odorous as the cedars of Lebanon. I only regret that you did not publish any more from the same source. In my next, I will mention some others from amongst your poems which have delighted me and let you know where I have been reading lately. Perhaps you would like to learn what books I am in the habit of looking into, and how far my tastes agree with yours. You could then *certainly* set me right.

I rarely meet with Mr Joseph Harpur now: his parliamentary duties seem to engross nearly the whole of his time. He is one of the purest-minded men I have ever met with. I know Mr Stenhouse: he introduced me to Henry Halloran a few weeks ago. The last-mentioned gentleman magnificently patronises me, and endeavours to impress upon me the 'fact' that it is a crime to write when you can't excel. What a pity it is that he don't follow up his theory in his own case, and leave me to take care of myself! I cannot find anything at all approximating to Genius in Halloran's or Evelyn's writings. Parkes had a poetical temperament evidently, and Michael is not so contemptible as interested critics would have him appear to be. Dr Woolley, a *crammed* man – a man who admires Tennyson by rote, and Browning backwards, is another of my would-be patrons. I have cut them all.

Thanking you for your kind letter, and hoping you will reply to this, when you have leisure, I remain

Yours Respectfully
Henry Kendall

Charles Harpur to Henry Kendall

Euroma, Gulph Diggings
9th Nov 1863

My dear Kendall,
Your two last came duly to hand.
As you say, I have no doubts but that the Herald *is* the best medium for literary publication – and anything that I may wish to see in print, I will from time to time send through you for insertion in that journal – viz: some further papers on Versification (in general); some other prose pieces; and now and then a poem or two. These poems (you may explain this to the Herald folk) will not *always* be original, but they will be *better* – that is, they will be as *finished* as I can make them.

• CORRESPONDENCE •

I am glad that our old friend Stenhouse was pleased with the paper on Blank Verse. His approval of a thing of the kind is of more value in my estimation, than that of all the rest of our literary judges bunched together. But I think he knows this. Next to his in value would be Dan Deniehy's; and next to Deniehy's in some things, *yours*.

I live a very solitary life here – utterly solitary, except so far as I am mixed up very unpleasantly with the petty fretting disputes &c. of that most contentious class of men – our diggers. They sometimes make me almost a man-dispiser – so grasping are they – so unfraternal & dishonest. And it almost always so happens that when I would devote an hour to all serene & beautiful things, their calls upon me as a Commissioner, are most frequent & exacting.

Whenever I enclose you any 'copy', you may take it for granted that I wish to see it in print.

Yours most truly
Chas: Harpur

Henry Kendall to Charles Harpur

Surveyor General's Office
April 29th 1865

My dear Mr Harpur,
Many domestic troubles have hindered me from writing back to you before this date. I have received at different times the newspapers for which I thank you. I do not like your new readings of your older poems at all times, but the latest draft of the blank verse fragment 'To A Comet' is *capital*. I like the epithet 'gipsy' in the recent version of the '*Master Mariner's Songs*', but in other respects you cannot well overcome any prejudice in favour of the lyric as it stands for us, in the published volume. There is at all times a charm about the rough rock that we cannot discover in the polished masonwork. Nevertheless I know you are right in the main; for the true poet is a sleepless artist. Yet you must forgive me for my overfear lest the 'freshness of the morning prime' should be sullied in the least where it is so pure and so abundant.

Let '*The Tower of the Dream*' stand for us as we know it. Never doubt its immortality; but, for the sake of hereafter delights, keep a jealous watch over its present integrity. I believe it is the highest result of your genius. It is even a Wonder Dream more wondrous than '*Kubla Khan*'.

When I read a poem once and remember it (through that one reading only) my faith in its beauty is thereafter established forever. I cannot forget '*Dora*, the gentle and the good'. The wordless '*Eva Grey*' is, to me, a continual face alight with the shining patience of perpetual pain. Have you not heard, in your forest walks, a wild broken wind, which after a day of shattered life, had fallen down to its softer evening passages? Have you not heard then a recurring sound forever like the sound of a fitful Aeolian Harp? You *have*, and therefore, '*Gramachree*', full of the 'red' sunset and perplexed with a perplexing sorrow was written. Its beauty makes the heart ache.

Excuse haste and paper. Just now I was scribbing this in face of an antithesis. The fellows in this office, with the exception of our old friend, Halloran, are a hopeless set. I have managed to get hold of the 1845 collection of *Sonnets* headed '*Thoughts*'. They are all familiar to me, and I have heretofore spoken to you of them. As I grow older my faith in your genius takes a deeper growth, even though I sometimes carp, like a critic.

When an opportunity occurs I will write to you concerning another matter. They print your contributions after a vile fashion in the '*Moruya Messenger*'. Why will you not send them to the '*Sydney Mail*'?

I have seven shillings of yours in hand. You[r] brother objected to take them, and suggested that I should wait till you come to Sydney. I am waiting a long time.

> Believe me,
> Yours, Faithfully.
> Henry Kendall.

Charles Harpur to Henry Kendall

> Euroma,
> 10th June, 1866

My dear Kendall,
If you knew how lonely I am here, I think you would write to me somewhat oftener than you do. There is not a single soul within thirty miles of me, that I care even to talk with – or *to*. How is dear old Stenhouse? What sort of a chap is Dr Brereton? How much taller does Halloran stand in his stockings since he became the Secretary's secretary? You see, you could tell me lots of things: and thereby provoke me, perhaps, to tell *you* lots of things in return. Still, if you really have not time, I am content to take the will for the deed.

I do not continue to send you the 'rag' you wot of – having become tired of publishing my 'things' in it, even with the view that I think I told you I had in doing so. – I should like, had I the means, to publish (as you once suggested) a vol: for the English Critics: for I know well enough, that I have long left all my Australian critics – many a year ago – standing

• CORRESPONDENCE •

hopelessly behind me, and mostly, too, upon the lowermost ledges of
Parnassus. But this, in one sense, is my misfortune. I have not the means,
however, to publish on my 'own hook', as a gild-digger would phrase it.
    I never see anything of yours now. Why is this?
    The period of my official life is running short – ending with the present
month. Whether the set now in power, will prolong it in any way, remains
to be seen.
    If you should see Maddock the Bookseller, be good enough to mention,
as from me, that I will settle with him in a short time.

Yours very truly,
Chas: Harpur

Charles Harpur to Henry Kendall

Euroma, via Bodalla
7th July, 1866

My dear Kendall,
'Telegonus' came duly to hand. I like it upon the whole. There are, to my
thinking, some very happy lines in it. But you could have made the verse
better, with better models, for your skill in versification is generally
somewhat remarkable. 'Telegonus', however, wants variety of pause and
cadence. You say yourself that it is not Tennysonian; but it might easily be
better. Tennyson's blank verse is always chargeable with a similar defect –
a want of *numerosity*; not, mind you, a slip-slop or piggled interflow of
parts, but a nicely varied cadential one. But, generally, in Tennyson's
verses of all kinds, – when not *sweet*, as in lyrical pieces, – there is a
feebleness, or I might say, *feminineness* of movement and flow. I cannot
call to mind a really thundrous line that he has written – such as either of
the following:

> 'Hurled heàdlong, flàming from the ethereal sky,
> With hideous ruin and combustion, dòwn
> To bottomless perdition.'

Study Milton & Wordsworth for a blank verse style, and combine the
master-movements of the two. Wordsworth will teach you how to loosen
& modernise Milton's, so as to make it more eloquent; and Milton will
show you how to put thunder into Wordworth's.
    I recd. a *private* letter from Parkes that shows I think that I have little to
expect from the present Cabinet. The fellow presumes to lecture me upon
some 'freaks', as he calls them – matters of minor morals manners with
which no Government have aught to do; and with which no manly

Government would condecend to become acquainted – through spies or volunteer informers, characters always base detestable – but no more base & detestable than those who employ and listen to them. This fellow Parkes! who has himself done things that would have hanged an honester and less subtle man! This fellow, I say, who has not even two qualifications for the high office he now fills, unless the profoundest hypocrisy be one, and preeminency in failure another!

The Secretary's secretary's note to you made me 'laugh consumedly' as Scrub says in the Play. What a prig it is. And only that the note is a private one *to you*, I would make it the theme of some lines that should render him a laughing-stock for life. He is not worth talking about.

Do you ever see my brother Joe? For some reason, he will not let *me* know anything of his present whereabouts or doings. Do you then, like a good fellow, tell me whatever you may know about him.

Don't forget to send me the Herald containing the 'Forging of the armour of Achilles' – if they publish it. It is my intention to try and get a literary engagement with Fairfax: for I must supplement my present means in some such way. I have, it is true, a snug well-furnished house over my head, with a good farm for its size; but I am otherwise poor, and have a large and helpless family. Hence I must now see what my pen will do for me.

Yours very truly
Chas: Harpur

Charles Harpur to Henry Kendall

Euroma
19th Jan/67

My dear Kendall,
How happens it that you have not written to me at all since your official promotion? Of which, however, I wish you joy.

The things I send you for publication in the Herald, are evidently inserted therein as it were with a grudge, or unwillingly. It would almost seem as if Fairfax were ashamed to have them for nothing, and yet had not the heart to pay anything for them. If therefore, when you receive this, my last paper (on Chaucer) is not printed, will you be good enough to get it back: and let me know that you have done so?

So far as to all publication in the papers, it is my intention to 'shut up', for the next five or six years: when I hope to be able to put forth at my own expense a volume of three or four hundred pages, trusting thereafter to time for the sale of the edition.

If there is any subject on which you have anything particular to say to me, write in reply to this, and at length – as it is likely that this is nearly the last letter I shall write to you or to anybody else (except on matters of pure business) for several years to come: for I intend to withdraw myself entirely from the outward world for a long time: and during which time I shall attend solely, first to my farm, & secondly to a subject which I have chosen for an *epic*. I am engaged just now in founding a poem of considerable extent upon a Rabbinical tradition – the Widow of Hebron: and which is turning out quite to my satisfaction; magnificent as an oriental palace and terrible as a thunder-storm.

The only two things – a couple of Satires – full of scorn and wildfire, that I shall publish before shutting up, and which shall shortly appear, it would not be prudent for you to know anything about – that is of course prior to their publication.

I see the Government have given us poor devils – the sacked Gold Commissioners, a trifle of compensation for their loss of office. But if the number is so great as I think it is, amongst whom this sum of £1629 is to be apportioned, it is a trifling compensation truly! Well, 'Fate & Jenkins' are just now uppermost, and one must only '*grin*'.

Yours very truly
Chas: Harpur

Charles Harpur to Henry Kendall

Euroma, via Bodalla,
15th October, 1867

My dear Kendall,

I thought the first number of the Colonial Monthly flimsy enough; but the second is even contemptible: the poetic contents absolutely *infamous*. I have come to the conclusion therefore that it would be best for me not to mix up with any such affair. A thing so written for in the main, would weigh down into the mire even the songs of the Gods. I wish you therefore, to be so good as to withdraw or withhold my contributions from it. Do this for me, and upon my honor, it is the last trouble of the kind I will ever give you.

My broken resolve of some months ago was altogether the best and wisest I could have come to: namely, to have nothing more to do with Sydney Journals of any kind – or with publication of any kind, until I could come forth with a volume on my own account. And to this old resolve I now recur for good.

As the copies in your possession of certain of my poems, are the most perfect perhaps of any, it would be as well that you should send me them. The Personal Sonnets I wish back especially: because it is my intention to finally preserve of them, only such as happen to be poetic both in *subject* and treatment. I will in future lend no hand in the celebration of men whom I find to be faithless and selfish – mere human beeves. At all events, in my final publication, the only interest I shall regard is the *essential poetry* of the piece under consideration. Those that would have their end in associating or mixing me up with the present race of Australians, could only have a damaging effect in some way – even the best of my contemporaries being such a . . . lot: fellows that make one 'hang his head, to call himself a *man*'.

Yours ever truly
Chas: Harpur

• CORRESPONDENCE •

Sources

Ms references are to the Harpur Papers in the Mitchell Library (ML), or to HP (Harpur-Parkes Correspondence – ML); SP (N.D. Stenhouse Papers – ML); LK (Letters of H. C. Kendall – ML); AAC (Australian Autograph Collection, Manuscripts Collections, La Trobe Library, State Library of Victoria).

Charles Harpur – His Own Epitaph: SP, A100; The Dream by the Fountain: A87[1]; Final Note to the Miscellaneous Poems: C382; From Rosa or Sonnets of Love: C383; Note to The Lass of Eulengo: C376; To the Sonnet on the Fate of Poetic Genius in a Sordid Community: C376; To Myself, June 1855: C384; Note to a Republican Lyric: B78; This Southern Land of Ours: A87[1]; A Note on the Australian-born whites from The Kangaroo Hunt: A97; The Tree of Liberty: C376; Finality: C376; From The True Finality: C376; Self-liberty: A87[1]; Humanity: A97; My Own Poetry: A87[1]; Australia's First Great Poet: A87[1]; From Harpur's Lecture on Poetry: A92; Bible Poetry and Piety: A92; Talent and Genius: A92; Wordsworth's Poetry: A87[1]; Early and Late Art: A92; Review of a Poem by Kendall: A87[2]; To Twank: A96; Modern Poetry: C384; From The Nevers of Poetry: A87[1]; From Finish of Style: A87[1]; The Perfect Poet: A89; Andrew Marvell: C376; To the Criticlings of Doggreldom: C381; Poetical Egotism: C376; From Harpur's Lecture on Poetry: A92; The Tower of the Dream: A97; Words Are Deeds: A90; Asinine Loyalty and Abject Patriotism: A87[2]; True and False Glory: C376; Wellington: C380; Edmund Burke: A92; On the Repeal Movement in Ireland: C376; Whatever Is, Is Right: C376; A Bit of Prose in the Vein and after the Manner of the Hon. Robert Boyle: C376; Satire: C376; Marvellous Martin: C376; From The Temple of Infamy: A93; A Roguish Epigram: A87[2]; From Sonnets Dedicated to Australian Senators: A92; From Bits: C384; The Big (Bygone) Claims of the Big Squatters: C376; Bush Justice: A94; A Splendid Is Never a Happy Land: A92; On the Proposed Recurrence to Transportation: A95; Aboriginal Death Song: C384; My Sable Fair: C376; Charity: C376; The Great Fish of the Sea (See): C376; Providential Design: A92; Note to Have Faith: C382; From The Witch of Hebron: A Rabbinical Legend: A97; From Note to The Death of Shelley: C376; Life and Death: A87[1]; Happiness and Faith: A87[1]; The World and the Soul: A87[2]; Note to the Poem Called Geologia: A87[2]; The Silence of Faith: A89; Life Without and Within: A87[1]; A Similitude: A87[1]; A Flight of Wild Ducks: A90; A Summer Night Scene: A90; The Spouse of Infinitude: A97; Note to the Poem 'Early Summer': C382; Early Summer: A88; A Mid-Summer Noon in the Australian Forest: A97; Dawn in the Australian Forest: A97; Names of Colonial Birds: C380; The Scenic Part of Poetry: C380; A Coast View: A97; The Bush Fire: A87[1]; Preface to The Kangaroo Hunt: A97; A Storm in the Mountains: A97; The Creek of the Four Graves: A87[1]; Poetic Descriptions of Violent Death: C376; Eden Lost: A87[1]; Charles Harpur to Henry Parkes, 21 March 1844: HP, AL 131; Charles Harpur to Nicol D. Stenhouse, 2 July 1859: SP, A100; Charles Harpur to Nicol. D. Stenhouse, 12 November 1859: SP, ML Mss 27; Henry Kendall to Charles Harpur, 25

168

• SOURCES •

September 1862: LK, C199; Charles Harpur to Henry Kendall, 9 November 1863: LK, C199; Henry Kendall to Charles Harpur, 29 April 1865: LK, C199; Charles Harpur to Henry Kendall, 10 June 1866: AAC Ms 5100-5102; Charles Harpur to Henry Kendall, 7 July 1866: AAC Ms 5100-5102; Charles Harpur to Henry Kendall, 19 January 1867: LK, C199; Charles Harpur to Henry Kendall, 15 October 1867: AAC Ms 5100-5102.

Further Reading

Michael Ackland, 'Charles Harpur for a New Generation,' *Quadrant*, (1984), 65-71.
Michael Ackland, 'Charles Harpur's "The Bush Fire" and "A Storm in the Mountains": Sublimity, Cognition and Faith,' *Southerly*, 43 (1983), 459-74.
Michael Ackland, 'Charles Harpur's Republicanism', *Westerly*, 29 (1984), 75-88.
J. Normington-Rawling, *Charles Harpur, An Australian*, (Sydney: Angus & Robertson, 1962)
Elizabeth Perkins, (Ed.), *The Poetical Works of Charles Harpur*, (Sydney: Angus & Robertson, 1984).
Judith Wright, *Charles Harpur*, (Melbourne: Oxford University Press, 1977).